D1596585

THE NATURAL AND POLITICAL
HISTORY OF THE
STATE OF VERMONT

THE
NATURAL AND POLITICAL
HISTORY
OF THE
STATE of VERMONT

ONE OF THE UNITED STATES OF AMERICA

TO WHICH IS ADDED

AN APPENDIX

CONTAINING ANSWERS TO SUNDRY QUERIES
ADDRESSED TO THE AUTHOR

———•———

By IRA ALLEN, Esquire
MAJOR-GENERAL OF THE MILITIA IN THE STATE OF VERMONT

———•———

London:

PRINTED BY J.W. MYERS, NO. 2, PATERNOSTER-ROW
AND SOLD BY W.WEST, NO. 1, QUEEN'S-HEAD
PASSAGE, PATERNOSTER-ROW

1798

———•———

CHARLES E. TUTTLE COMPANY
RUTLAND, VERMONT

Representatives
Continental Europe: BOXERBOOKS, INC., *Zurich*
British Isles: PRENTICE-HALL INTERNATIONAL, INC., *London*
Australasia: PAUL FLESCH & CO., PTY. LTD., *Melbourne*
Canada: M. G. HURTIG LTD., *Edmonton*

Published by the Charles E. Tuttle Company, Inc.
of Rutland, Vermont & Tokyo, Japan
with editorial offices at Suido 1-chome, 2-6
Bunkyo-ku, Tokyo, Japan

Copyright in Japan, 1969, by Charles E. Tuttle Co., Inc.

Library of Congress Catalog Card No. 69-19611

International Standard Book No. 0-8048-0419-2

First Tuttle edition, 1969
Third printing, 1973

PRINTED IN JAPAN

TABLE OF CONTENTS

PUBLISHER'S FOREWORD

HISTORIES are the tangible links in time and tradition; the more links, the better understanding of an epoch and an age, a movement and a trend, a nation and a people.

This edition, taken from the *Collections of the Vermont Historical Society*, Vol. 1, Montpelier, 1870, is an important link in the history of the Green Mountain State. It describes the struggles and heartaches the people encountered in founding and establishing the independence of the State against the "intrigues and claims of New York, New Hampshire and Massachusetts."

Significantly, these early claims and jurisdictional disputes, and especially the one with New York, "tended much to sour the minds" of the other colonists against the British Government, inasmuch as the colonists believed that the Governor and Council of New York acted under instructions of the British Cabinet. Thus the Vermont dispute was instrumental in hastening the Revolution.

The author, despite adversity and great financial sacrifice, played a key role in the struggle for statehood. If his principal motive for the publication of his history was "to disabuse the public mind there in relation to a purchase by him of a quantity of arms in France, which had been captured by a British vessel," history has been the chief beneficiary. And historians generally agree that the purchase was for the Militia of the State of Vermont.

A brother of the famous Gen. Ethan Allen, Ira Allen was one of the unsung heroes of that stirring period. Thus it is with considerable pride and pleasure that the publisher presents this reprint on the 170th anniversary of the first London edition. This book was originally published in 1798 by J. W. Myers, London.

PRELIMINARY NOTE

THE following history of Vermont, by IRA ALLEN, possesses a peculiar interest from the fact that it treats largely of events in which the author was a prominent actor. It was written and published in England towards the close of the last century, and having become quite scarce it is thought worthy of being re-produced in this volume.

Ira Allen was the youngest of six brothers, of whom Col. Ethan Allen was the eldest, was born at Cornwall, Connecticut, May 1, 1751, and came to the New Hampshire Grants in 1772, when about twenty-one years of age. He had received a good common school education and was a practical land surveyor. He soon became one of the active leaders of the settlers in their struggles against the hostile measures of New York, and was afterwards prominent among the inhabitants of the territory in their resistance to the oppressions of the British crown, and also in their foundation of a state government and in maintaining its independence. He was a delegate to the several conventions of the people of the New Hampshire Grants preparatory to the organization of the state government, a member and Secretary to the Council of Safety that carried them successfully through the trying campaign of 1777, and when the government, under the Constitution, went into operation in 1778, he was elected one of the Governor's Council and State Treasurer, and the next year he became Surveyor-General, all of which offices he held by successive annual elections until about 1787. He was also frequently an agent of the state to the Continental Congress, and to several of the state governments, and was the principal negotiator of the truce with Canada in 1781 and 1782, which prevented the invasion of the state from that province, all of which missions he conducted with much skill and ability. Of these several matters his history gives a particular and interesting account.

It appears from Mr. Allen's preface that his principal motive for the preparation and publication of his history in England was to disabuse the public mind there in relation to a purchase by him of a quantity of arms in France, which had been captured by a British vessel, and about which a suit was then pending in the English Court of Admiralty. For the information of the general reader some account of this controversy seems necessary.

Mr. Allen's position as Surveyor-General had given him peculiar facilities for land speculations, in which he had extensively engaged. He held, or claimed to hold, title to very large quantities of lands, mostly in the northwesterly part of the state in the valley of Lake Champlain. He had a favorite project of increasing their value and promoting the interest of the state, by means of a ship canal to connect the waters of the St. Lawrence with that lake, of which, by application to the Governor of Canada, he procured the survey of a route to be made as early as 1785. This would seem to have been the germ of an undertaking which now, in 1870, promises to be successfully accomplished at no very distant day, by the common efforts of capitalists and railroad managers of the Eastern States and Canada.

Mr. Allen united great energy of purpose with a passion for speculation and adventure. In 1795 he conceived the project of going to Europe to further his scheme for a canal, to dispose of his lands, and to purchase a quantity of arms to supply the militia of the state, in which they were greatly deficient, and of about one-fourth of which he was in command as Major-General. Taking with him a certificate of his character, and of the honorable public positions he had held, he went to England, where he arrived in January, 1796, and soon had an interview with the Duke of Portland respecting the construction of the canal, but without any favorable result. He then went to Paris, where he appears to have disposed of some of his lands, and on the 11th of July, 1796, he concluded a contract with the French Directory for the purchase of " 20,000 muskets with bayonets, 24 brass four pound field-pieces, six gun-carriages and six cannon-waggons," declared in the written contract to be "for the use of the militia of the

State of Vermont." Most of the arms were delivered on board of the *Olive Branch*, an American vessel, at Ostend, a French port, from which the ship sailed for New York on the 11th of November, 1796, and on the 19th of the same month was captured by a British ship of war, carried into Portsmouth, England, and libeled in the Court of Admiralty as lawful prize.

France was at that time at war with England, but there was nothing in the acknowledged law of nations, or in any treaty, which forbid the exportation of arms from a belligerent power to a neutral port in a neutral vessel. The only ground on which the condemnation of the cargo could be claimed was that the contract was not real but collusive, and that instead of being intended for the Vermont militia, the arms were designed to be used in the interest of France against the territory and subjects of Great Britain. The proof produced by Mr. Allen was very strong in favor of the *bona fide* character of the transaction, and the captors could bring forward no direct evidence to counteract it. They however claimed that the circumstances under which the arms were obtained were inconsistent with a fair contract of purchase, and were of so suspicious a character as to demand their condemnation. By the written contract produced by Mr. Allen, it appeared that he was to pay twenty-five livres, or about five dollars, for each musket, and that one hundred thousand livres, or one-fifth of the purchase money, had been paid in cash, and that for the other four-fifths a credit, on the personal obligation of Mr. Allen, had been given him for seven years, on annual interest at the rate of five per cent.

France at this time was at war, not only with England, but with other European powers, had an army of invasion in Italy, and was maintaining on her north-eastern frontier a doubtful struggle with Austria. That the French government, at such a time, should sell to a stranger and foreigner such a quantity of arms, on such liberal terms of payment, to be carried out of the country, and especially to the United States, with which their relations were of a threatening character, was declared to be altogether improbable. The fairness of the transaction was violently assailed in London and other newspapers. It was charged that Mr. Allen had no authority from the State of Vermont to make the purchase, which was indeed true ; that he was " a Jacobin friend of France," employed by the Directory ; that the arms were intended to be used in a contemplated revolt against the British government in Canada, and were connected with an attempt of that kind alleged to have been fomented by Mr. Adel, the French Minister to the United States, and for which a Major McLane had been convicted of treason and executed at Quebec.   Mr. Allen replied to these charges with earnestness and ability, in newspaper and pamphlet publications, and in a volume of four hundred pages, entitled *The Olive Branch*, printed in London early in 1798, in which the evidence produced by him in the Court of Admiralty and the proceedings of said court were largely set forth.   He also prepared and published his History of Vermont, to show that the extent and population of the state was such as to need the arms he had obtained, and that his own relations and those of the people of the state, with the governing authorities of Canada, were of so friendly and confidential a character as to preclude the supposition that any hostile measures against that province could have been intended.

The Judge in Admiralty having, in December 1797, decided in favor of the captors, Mr. Allen appealed to a higher Court, and the proceedings were protracted at great trouble and expense to him until February, 1804, when the Appellate Court ordered the arms to be restored to him ; but, on the ground that there had been probable cause for their seizure, directed him to pay the costs of the captors.   These, together with his own costs and expenditures in the controversy, amounted to many thousands of dollars.   The arms, previous to the final decision, had been delivered to Mr. Allen on his procuring sufficient bonds to abide such decree as the Court should make respecting them, and had been sent to New York for sale for his benefit.   The consignees, without making any payment to him or rendering any account of their sales, became bankrupt, and this, with his other losses and expenditures, involved him in pecuniary difficulties and embarrassments, from which he was never afterwards able to extricate himself.   He returned to Vermont for short periods, but left the state in the fall of 1804, and thereafter continued to reside in Philadelphia, where he died January 7, 1814.

In 1805, Mr. Allen published in Philadelphia another volume of

over five hundred pages, entitled *The Olive Branch*, giving a
further account of the proceedings, and treating also of other
personal as well as historical and political matters. He also
published in Philadelphia, in 1807, a pamphlet containing some
additional comments on the Olive Branch controversy, and relating also to controversies and pecuniary difficulties of his with
some Vermonters and others. From these several publications
the foregoing accounts have been compiled.

Although it cannot be denied that the purpose for which the
arms were obtained by Mr. Allen from the French Government
was liable to some degree of suspicion, yet it is difficult to
read the great mass of evidence produced by him to show the
fairness of the transaction, without being convinced that his real
object was to furnish the militia of Vermont with arms, of which
they were greatly deficient, and with which each individual was
required by law to supply himself under the penalty of a considerable fine. Mr. Allen expected to be able to dispose of the
arms on such reasonable terms as to secure their ready sale, and
at the same time at such an advance on their cost as to make it a
successful and profitable pecuniary speculation. This he probably would have done, if the passage of his vessel to New York
had not been interrupted.

One of the principal objects of Mr. Allen in his history having
been to defend himself before the English public against charges
of a design to excite an insurrection and revolt in Canada, he
would be personally interested, to represent that his own relations
and those of the people of Vermont with the government of that
province, were of the most friendly and intimate character. Perhaps what he says on that subject should for that reason be taken
with some degree of allowance.

Mr. Allen apologizes in his preface for any inaccuracies of dates
and for other minor errors in his history, on account of its having
been prepared when he was " remote from original documents "
and under peculiar embarrassments. Some of these errors are
noticed and corrected in the following reprint in brief foot notes,
which notes are referred to by figures and included in brackets to
distinguish them from those in the original work, which are
marked in the usual manner.

PREFACE

ONE reason amongst others that led to the publication of this memoir, was the proceedings of the High Court of Admiralty of England, relative to twenty thousand muskets with their bayonets, twenty-four brass four-pound field-pieces, six gun-carriages, and six cannon-waggons, purchased at Paris, in July, 1796, by the Author, from the French Government, for the equipment of the militia in the State of Vermont, in America, according to the written request of Thomas Chittenden, Governor and Captain General of said State, in 1795. Those arms being thus purchased, the ship Olive Branch, a neutral bottom, was chartered in London to convey them to New York; she received her cargo at Ostend, and on the 11th of November, 1796, sailed from that Port for New York, and on the 19th of the same month, was taken by his Majesty's ship of war the Audacious, Davidge Gould, Esq; Commander, in latitude 47 7 north, and longitude 10 41 west from the meridian of London, and brought to Portsmouth, and soon after libelled by the Captors in the High Court of Admiralty at London, where the Author of the following pages laid in his claim to the cargo in due form of law. In the course of this cause the character of the people of Vermont and that of the claimant were frequently called in question, which operated as a stimulus to this publication.

The public are therefore most respectfully referred to the " Particulars of the capture of the ship Olive Branch, laden with a cargo of arms, &c. the property of Major General Ira Allen, destined for supplying the militia of Vermont, and captured by his Britannic Majesty's ship of war Audacious, together with the proceedings and evidence before the High Court of Admiralty of Great Britain, Vol. I. by Ira Allen, Esq; of Vermont, in the United States of America, the claimant in this cause, and printed by J. W. Myers, No. 2, Paternoster-Row, London, 1798."

The aim of the writer has been to lay open the source of contention between Vermont and New York, and the reasons which induced the former to repudiate both the jurisdiction and claim of the latter, before and during the American revolution, and also to point out the embarrassments the people met with in founding and establishing the independence of the State against the intrigues and claims of New York, New Hampshire, and Massachuseets, supported as they were by repeated resolves of Congress ; when they were exposed to the power of a British army in Canada, &c.

Thus surrounded on every side, when their numbers were small, without affluence, and in a perilous situation ; necessity, the mother of invention, instituted policy in place of power, which the author attempts to explain, but for want of documents and certain political expedients, some matters will be omitted till a future edition (in Vermont).

To state from memory historical facts relative to Vermont, many years past, with precision and correctness of dates, remote from original documents, is not to be expected, especially from a person involved in mercantile concerns, and embarrassed in a suit of much consequence ; VI when Europe is affected with continental revolutions, and America feels the consequence ; under such circumstances the Author relies on the public indulgence to pardon and correct all errors and inevitable imperfections, until they may be noted in a future impression.

Many of the principal actors in establishing the independence of Vermont being numbered with the dead, the writer considered it his duty, while detained in this country, to spend a few weeks in relating the various manœuvres made use of to perfect the constitution and Government of Vermont, which equally defends the rights and liberties of all.

Hereafter it may be proper further to explain the proceedings of New York against Vermont, as they were literally contrary to the orders of the King and Privy Council, and as they laid the foundation for the independence of Vermont. The conduct of the late colony of New York tended much to sour the minds of other colonists against the Government of Great Britain, believing as they did, that the Governor VII and Council of New York acted in conformity to instructions from the British Cabinet. The principles of the controversy between New York and Vermont were spread and well understood in the colonies several years before the American war began, and no doubt had considerable influence in hastening and bringing about the revolution of America.

An appendix has been formed and subjoined to answer a number of queries of a gentleman respecting the general state of the country, its productions and habits.

The AUTHOR.

NATURAL and POLITICAL

HISTORY

OF

VERMONT

THE territory forming the present independent State of Vermont, is situate between 42° 45' and 45 degrees of north latitude, and between 3° 53' and 5° 46' of longitude, east of the city of Washington, which corresponds with 71° 22' and 73° 15' west of London, and 73° 47' and 75° 40' of longitude west from Paris. It is bounded at the east on the west bank of Connecticut River, which is the western bounds of New Hampshire; on the north by the south line of Lower Canada; on the west by the waters of Lake Champlain, East Bay, and up Poultney River where it intersects the west line of Poultney; thence by a strait line to the north west corner of Massachusett; and thence east on the north line of Massachusett to Connecticut River. Its length measured by the latitude is one hundred and fifty-six miles and three-eight's of a mile; its north line is ninety miles and one-fourth, and its south is forty-one miles. Its mean breadth is nearly sixty-five miles, which gives 10,164 superficial square miles and three-eighths, or 6,505,200 acres. The lands included within the State are fertile and well calculated for agriculture; the soil, with few exceptions, is deep, rich, moist, loamy, warm, and of a dark colour and loose contexture; wheat, Indian corn, and other kinds of grain grow and flourish luxuriantly as soon as the woods are removed, without the use of the plough; and after the first crop naturally produces grass for grazing and mowing. The face of the country affords different aspects; the lands adjoining the rivers are extensive fine plains and meadows; at a distance they rise into hills and mountains with many beautiful and productive valleys between them; springs and streams issue from those hills and mountains, which plentifully supply and fertilize the earth. The Green Mountains begin in Canada near the Bay of Chaleur, and one branch runs through Vermont, Massachusett, and Connecticut, and ends near New Haven. Their general course is from N. N. east to S. S. west, and they divide Vermont nearly in the centre; from ten to fifteen miles in width, and are the reservoirs of water to supply the adjacent hills and country; they are principally cloathed with spruce, hemlock, firs, some pine, and other ever greens. The whole range is composed of huge

3   rocks confusedly piled on one another, though in many places are large inlets of excellent land, which will be of more value for grazing than the low country, as they are but seldom exposed to droughts, and the grass is more nutritious. The humidity and height of these mountains render the air several degrees colder than it is in the flat country. The greatest height of Killington Peak (according to Dr. Williams) is 3454 feet above the level of the ocean, and the highest mountain within the State, whose summit has been taken by actual mensuration; though it is concluded the Camel's Rump and Mansfield Mountain, if measured, would be found to exceed that,[1] yet not more than half the height of the *White Hills*, the highest mountains in New England, which are said to be about 7,800 feet[2] above the level of the sea, and but a little below the line of perpetual congelation in the same latitude in Europe.* Lake Champlain separates Vermont from the State of New York; its length (reckoning from *White Hall*,† in the State of New York, to Fort St. Johns, in Lower Canada) is about one hundred and sixty miles, and its mean width near five miles. It contains three valuable islands which are within the jurisdiction of Vermont, viz. the north and south heroes, and La Motte. Lake Mumphramagog is about forty miles long and nearly

4   three miles broad; its greatest part lies in Lower Canada; the division line at latitude 45° crosses it; the lands and timber circumjacent to it are principally good, though at present the former is but partially cultivated. It discharges itself into the River St. Lawrence at the north, through the River St. Francois and Lake St. Peters; its navigation is more impeded by rapids

---

*44° 15'.   † Formerly Skeensborough.

[1] [By the report of the Geological Survey of the state, made in 1859, Vol. II, p. 876, it appears that the height of the three mountains above the ocean is as follows:

     Mount Mansfield...................................4348 feet.
     Killington Peak...................................4180 "
     Camel's Hump.....................................4083 "]

[2] [6634 feet.—*Mitchell.*]

and falls than the River Sorel is from St. John's to Chamble, through which Champlain empties into St. Lawrence.

In 1785 Captain Twist made a survey and level to ascertain the expence of a canal from the River St. Lawrence to Lake Champlain. By his report it is said to appear that the sum of twenty-seven thousand pounds sterling would make a canal sufficient for a ship of 200 tons to pass into Lake Champlain, which would extend a navigation 180 miles into the country, and make Lake Champlain a port; an idea which Congress have already anticipated, by the actual establishment of a custom-house at Alburg, near the entrance of the Lake.

The Rivers Missisqui, La Moile, and Onion, on the west side of the Green Mountains, flow into Champlain, and are of considerable extent. Otter Creek would be called a river in Europe, being equal in magnitude to either of the rivers beforementioned; so 5 would many other streams which have not that appellation, though much larger than the *Isis*, so highly celebrated by the poets of Oxford. The Missisqui rises in Kellyvale, and runs north across the south line of Canada, thence turning S. westerly re-enters Vermont at Richford, and after a course of about seventy miles, discharges itself into Missisqui Bay at Highgate. This meandring river is navigable for large boats to Swanton Falls. La Moile and Onion Rivers are nearly of the same extent, and run in a serpentine manner. Otter Creek flows in a northward course nearly 90 miles, and unites with Champlain at Ferrisburg; large vessels go up eight miles to the falls at Vergennes. The rivers and streams on the east side of the Green Mountains are more numerous, but of less magnitude, than those on the west, and all of them fall into Connecticut River; the most considerable are West River, White River, and Posoomsuck. The surface of the country appears to have undergone various changes. Large trunks of trees have been found in some places as low as thirty feet under the earth, which, no doubt, have lain there for ages, and from various circumstances, it is evident they once flourished above the spot where they lie. The floods, from time to time, have changed the beds of several of our rivers, as the different strata at twenty, thirty, and forty feet below the surface evince ; and there is reason to conclude that the intervals have thereby been formed. The operation of water upon solid rocks indicates a very remote period, and proves they have been long subject to the power of that ele-6 ment, which has worn holes, of different forms, and a depth that astonishes the human mind. Travellers often have paid attention to the perforated rocks in Black River, at Cavendish.

About three miles from Burlington Bay, the River Onion presents a singular contraction, about seventy-five feet in breadth,
depth unknown. Two rocks rise at this point on each side, opposite
to each other, which pointed out the ease of making a wooden
bridge across it, ninety feet above the water, and which has been
found exceedingly convenient to passengers. Above and below
this narrow place, the water is computed to be eighty-seven yards
in breadth. How or in what manner this happened is a question
worthy the enquiry of the naturalist, especially, when we view a
channel south of this river which resembles the old bed of one,
and if so, hence it is probable to conjecture, that the fertile lands,
for several miles up said river, might have once been the bed of a
lake, which supposition is farther strengthened by the following
curious fact, well authenticated :——

At Judge Lane's, in digging a well near the said river, at the
depth of twenty-four feet, wood was found, and about thirty frogs
were discovered, but so apparently petrified that it was difficult to
distinguish them from so many small stones. When brought out of
the well, disengaged from the earth, and exposed to the air,
they gradually felt the vivifying beams of the sun, and, to
the surprize of all present, leaped away with as much animation as
if they had never lain in their subterraneous prison. The place
where this well was sunk, was on high grounds, often surrounded
by the river in flood times; large pines, and the ancient fragments
of them, are found on this land; from the appearance of the
growth of this timber, those frogs we may well suppose to have
remained under ground six hundred years. To account for this
phenomenon, we must suppose some convulsion of nature to have
buried those animals thus deep, whilst in a torpid state, and thus
being excluded from the air, continued in the state in which they
were found.

The River Onion, in passing through the range of the Green
Mountains, also exhibits another curiosity :——A stone bridge,
consisting of one entire fragment, over which a man may pass,
and which appears to have been separated from a perpendicular
rock on the south side, two hundred feet high. Above and below
this place, the water may be about one hundred yards in breadth.
The river flows underneath this bridge in low water, but when
swelled with floods, runs over.

In the spring of 1783, the dissolving snow and heavy rains
swelled the River Poultney to such an extraordinary height, that

8 it broke its usual bounds at Fair-haven, whence it rushed with such impetuosity through a pine plain as to form a new channel, which is the less surprizing, as the soil was of a light texture on a stratum of hard blue clay, which it even wore away with such force as to discolour the water upwards of four months, sometimes extending to Crown Point, a course of fifty miles. It soon deserted Colonel Clark's intended mill, seat, and fall, and poured so rapid a torrent as to undermine and carry off lofty pines, the tops of which, when fallen in, and held by the roots, did not fathom the bottom. What is strange, logs of wood were found in the banks, thirty feet beneath the surface of the soil, and different layers of earth, at different depths. It is not easy to account for these circumstances. Let us suppose for a moment, that the present interval above this fall, was once the bed of a lake, through which the river ran, and that in the order of nature, and the course of time, wood, sand, &c. carried down by floods, choaked up the lake. The waters being no longer retained in their usual reservoir, rolled with all their strength, the effects of which, at length, disclosed the materials of its original bed.

Vermont contains almost every thing within itself that can contribute to the immediate wants, convenience, and even luxury of 9 man. This State abounds with different kinds of iron ore, well suited for hollow ware, bar-iron, and steel, together with lead and copper ore, ochre, red and yellow, lime-stone, and marble, white and beautifully clouded; and other kind of building stone : different sorts of clay for bricks, &c. materials from which putty of a good quality is made; springs which produce salts equal to that of Epsom; white pitch, yellow pine, oak, white, red, and black; and other species of useful timber, amongst which is the sugar maple, from which the farmers often make more sugar than serves for the usual consumption of their families, by the use of their kitchen utensils; good hops and grapes grow spontaneously in the uncultivated intervals; apples, pears, plumbs, damascenes, red, black, and choke cherries, currants, gooseberries, rasberries, strawberries, melons, squashes, pompkins, &c. rise to great perfection in open fields and gardens.

The climate of Vermont is friendly to population and longevity; the air is salubrious, notwithstanding it partakes of heat and cold in high degrees*, which gradually make their approaches. The

* The extremes of heat and cold may be considered by Farenheit's thermometer; greatest height 94°, least height 27° below, and the mean

frosts commonly retire about the 20th of April and return in October.   Their first appearance is on the low lands in the congelation of the dews and vapours.   High winds are found to
prevent the humidity of the night falling on the earth, and fogs
retain so much heat as to defeat the bad effects of a frost on vegetables and fruit.   From the latter part of December to the last of
March the snow covers the low lands from one to two feet in
depth, and the mountains from two to four.   It remains longer
on the mountains than the valleys and hills.   As soon as the
snows melt off the mountains, the earth appears to be fertilized,
and vegetation comes on rapidly; with a little cultivation the
ground is prepared to receive the seed, and the vegetables soon
spring forth to perfection.

The severity of the winter seldom kills young trees, or freezes
any of the cattle, although they are not housed; nor is the cold
so affecting to the inhabitants as the extremes and sudden trans-
ition from heat to cold on the sea coasts; there is a steady, settled frost, for three months, and generally with little variation;
the people, being accustomed to it, dress accordingly, and are far
more healthy during this season than those who are subject to the
vicissitudes of heat and cold near the ocean.

The most prevalent winds are west, north west, and northerly;
they are dry and elastic.   Those from the south and south west
are warm and more relaxing.   The weather is generally fair
in winter.   The snows are frequent, and for the most part
fall in small quantities, without high winds.   Rain is uncommon
in the winter, but hail is not.   In April and May the weather
becomes mild, attended with frequent showers, which promote vegetation.   Though the weather, during the summer months, is generally clear and settled, yet it has been found, by meteorological
observations, that near double the quantity of rain falls in Vermont to what falls in the same parallel of latitude in Europe.
Naturalists attribute this to the forests and the uncultivated state
of the country, which furnish more water for the formation of
clouds, but notwithstanding this opinion, many parts of America
suffer more from droughts than any part of Europe.

The heat in the middle of the summer days is often uncomfort-
able, though the nights are cool and agreeable.   The weather

heat, according to three years observations by Dr. Williams, in latitude
43° 38', at 43° one-half, and which is more than 10° degrees below the
mean heat of the cells of the Observatory at Paris.

from the 15th of May to the 20th of October is, on the whole,
very pleasant. Thunder and lightening are frequent in May,
June, July, and August. The *Aurora Borealis* is the most common in March, September, and October, but is not unusual at
other times of the year.

The climate admits of melioration as the woods are cleared
away. The want of accurate meteorological observations pre-
12 vents our determining whether the rain has decreased in the
same proportion with the snow : Certain it is, that the snow
has decreased in a very visible manner since settling and clearing
the lands, in many parts of the State. Perhaps the decrease of
snow and rain will keep pace with the temperature of the atmos-
phere, which, in a century and a half (according to Dr. Williams)
has changed for the better, between ten and twelve degrees,
though at present about ten or twelve degrees colder than in the
same latitude in Europe. Many of the small springs, streams, and
brooks, have dried up ; miry places and large swamps have been
converted into the richest meadows and arable lands. One of the
first effects of cultivation is the dissipation of the waters, and a
change in the swampy soil to that of dry and fertile lands. The
forests abound with almost innumerable kinds of trees, shrubs,
and vines ; among the former, (reckoning the most useful) are
the pine, cedar, maple, oak, ash, hickory, and wild cherry. Many
vegetables are indigenous, and possessed of sanative qualities in a
high degree, as far as has been proved in their application to
medicinal purposes.

Various kinds of quadrupeds, peculiar to a northern and cold
climate, are found in Vermont. Dr. Williams enumerates thirty-
six. According to that able naturalist, Count de Buffon, there
are seventy-five in America peculiar to it, and twenty-five which
13 are not, making in the whole one hundred. He concludes,
that there are about two hundred diffused over the face of
the globe. Vermont is not less fruitful in birds and fishes, than
in the four-footed race.

The extensive lakes and rivers in Vermont, and those contiguous thereto, are abundantly stored with fish, which in magnitude,
variety, and flavour, equal, and in many respects excel those of
the same species in Europe, particularly sturgeon, salmon, salmon-
trout, muskinunge, pike, &c. and in Davis and Lester Lakes,
trouts are often taken from 20 to 30lbs. weight, with a line from
70 to 100 feet in length. Nature is not less bountiful to this
State in fowl and quadrupeds of different kinds. The most useful

ful in the first class are wild geese and ducks, partridge, pheasant, wild-pigeon, quail, &c. In the second, moose-deer, bear, beaver, hare, rabbit, otter, &c. independent of a large and increasing stock of domestic animals. Hunting, fishing, and fowling, are free to all orders, in all seasons, except the killing of deer from the beginning of January to the first of September, as in part of that interval the skin and carcass are not so valuable ; the intent of the other part of this law (founded on nature) is to preserve the young till they can exist without the dam.

In 1741, the line, called the east and west line, which was the boundary between the provinces of New Hampshire and Massachusett, was ran and established. This line extended southward further than had been imagined, and included in New Hampshire the fort called Fort Dummer, which had been built and garrisoned by Massachusett's, but afterwards was supported at the joint expence of both provinces, as a mutual defence against the inroads of the savages, as the adjacent country, at the commencement of the war in 1754, was nearly a wilderness. A few families settled at and near this fort, as early as 1724, contiguous to Connecticut River, on locations from and under the Province of Massachusett, which lands were afterwards granted by Benning Wentworth, Governor of the Province of New Hampshire, in townships of six miles square each, by the names of Hinsdale, Brattleboro', and Fulham ; and the dispute about the lands and titles was accommodated. A few Dutch families settled on the banks of Hoosoock River, without any titles to the lands, and which were afterwards granted by the Governor of New Hampshire, under the name of Pownal. Near the south line of this township were two block forts erected by Massachusett's to guard the frontiers against the Indians and Canadians, whose incursions were dangerous. In 1731, the French erected the garrisons of Ticonderoga and Crown Point, and commenced settlements on Seignoral Grants, contiguous to Lake Champlain ; the most flourishing of these was a settlement upon a point called Chimney Point, opposite to Crown Point, upon the said lake.[1] On the Missisqui River was a large Indian town, which became greatly depopulated about 1730, by a mortal sickness that raged among them ; in consequence of which they evacuated the place, according to the tradition of the savages, and settled on the River St. Francoise, to get rid of *Hoggomog*, (the devil) leaving their beautiful fields, which extended four miles on the river, waste.

14

15

---

[1] [The French began their fortifications at Ticonderoga in 1755. *Col. His. N. Y.*, Vol. VI, p. 1001, 1003, 1021.]

In

In pursuance to orders and instructions from his Britannic Majesty and the Privy Council, the Governor of New Hampshire (Benning Wentworth) proceeded, in 1749, to grant the lands on the west of Connecticut River, and north of the division line between the two Provinces, to such persons as would settle on and cultivate the same; those grants went under the title of *New Hampshire Grants*, each grant being six miles square, to sixty-eight proprietors, in equal shares, whose names were entered on the charter, reserving to himself 500 acres at the corner of every township, which were considered as two shares. Also reserving four public rights, viz. one to the Society for the propagation of the Gospel in foreign parts, one for a perpetual glebe to the Church of England, as by law established, one for the first settled Minister of the Gospel in the town, and one for the benefit of a School. The patentees or possessors after ten years were to pay ninepence sterling per annum on each and every hundred acres, as quit-rent to his Majesty. Each township was erected into a corporation, and authorized to act as such; and so soon as fifty families were settled therein, they were to have the privilege of a fair.

16 It is to be remembered, that Governor Wentworth made about one hundred and forty grants on similar principles, between 1749 and 1764, yet few settlements were made on them till after the capture of Montreal in 1761, and the reduction of Canada. In the course of this war, the French abandoned their patents, burnt their houses, and removed to Canada with the Indians, who had been a heavy scourge to the frontiers of New England, from its first settlement in 1620. Many of the patentees on the New Hampshire Grants, passed through the wilderness as soldiers, in the war against Canada; a road was cut from No. 4, (Charlestown) on Connecticut River, to Crown Point; others had traversed those woods as hunters and scouting parties, by which means they discovered the beauties of the country, and the richness of the soil; a country that had been hitherto reserved by contending nations as a barrier, and proved a snare for the subjects of both. At the happy period when Canada and New England became subject to one king, this wilderness was rapidly settled, and soon changed into fruitful fields and pleasant gardens, as there were no longer any savages to make the inhabitants afraid.

"To check the proceedings of New Hampshire, and to intimidate the settlers, Mr. Colden, Lieutenant Governor of New York, 17 issued a proclamation*, reciting the grants to the Duke of York, asserting their validity, claiming the jurisdiction as far east

* 1763, December 8th.

cast as Connecticut River, and commanding the Sheriff of the County of Albany to make a return of the names of all persons who, under colour of the New Hampshire Grants, had taken possession of any lands to the west of the river.

"To prevent the effects that might arise from this proclamation, the Governor of New Hampshire put forth another proclamation*, declaring the grant to the Duke of York to be obsolete ; that New Hampshire extended as far to the west as Massachusett's and Connecticut; that the grants made by New Hampshire would be confirmed, if the jurisdiction should be altered ; the setlers were exhorted not to be intimidated, but to be industrious and diligent in cultivating their lands ; and civil officers were required to exercise jurisdiction as far westward as grants had been made, and to punish all disturbers of the peace."

Their prosperity and happy situation raised the envy of a number of avaricious and designing men in the colony of New York, who devised ways and means to change the jurisdiction, and attempted to dispossess the inhabitants and proprietors of their property. Their plan was curious as it was culpable. In 1763, 18 strangers were observed to pass through the district of the New Hampshire Grants, under the pretence of speculating in lands, but it was known that under this pretext they carefully took down the names of the inhabitants. Soon after, a petition to his Majesty and the Privy Council was made out, as was supposed, signed with the names of the settlers, and sent to London, praying that the district, lying west of Connecticut River, might be annexed to the Colony of New York, in consequence of its local situation, as best calculated to promote trade ; and that the western bank of Connecticut River might be appointed the eastern boundary thereof. The petition had its effect; for on July the 20th, 1764, an order passed in council, declaring the western bank of Connecticut River, opposite the Province of New Hampshire, to be of right the eastern boundary of New York. The jurisdiction being changed by his Majesty's order, and the reasons not known, the people on the grants under New Hampshire acquiesced, never entertaining an idea that the title of their lands would be called in question, when both were royal governments. The Governor of New Hampshire remonstrated against this loss of territory, and represented it to be injurious to the settlement and peace of the country ; but his council being contracted in their politics, and more fond of gratifying the over-bearing influence of the favourite colony

* 1764, March 13th.

of

of New York, than of the just remonstrance of their Governor,
19 induced his Excellency, of course, to relinquish all civil and
military government over his grants west of the Connecticut
River; and in his proclamation, he recommended to the proprietors and settlers *submission and due obedience to the authority
and laws of the colony of New York*, whereupon the Governor of
New York issued his proclamation, claiming the jurisdiction, and
requiring the inhabitants to deliver up their New Hampshire
titles, and take out new grants of their lands, which was to be
granted the settlers upon paying half the usual fees. Civil and
military officers were accordingly appointed among the people of
the New Hampshire Grants, and every thing seemed to presage
happiness and prosperity. But their prospects were soon clouded; for the Governor of the colony of New York, who, with the
advice of his council, on seeing the people not disposed to
purchase their own lands over again, proceeded to re-grant
the lands which they already held under the grant of one
Royal Governor, whose authority was equal to that of any
other Royal Governor. Fees of office, rather than justice or
sound policy, actuated the Governor of New York, as will appear
in the sequel; for certain of his favorites, who had distinguished
themselves in procuring the change of jurisdiction, obtained extensive grants of other people's property. This conduct alarmed
the settlers, not knowing what measures were best to secure their
common interest; all being willing to own the jurisdiction of New
20 York, but none being disposed to yield their lands; they
therefore remonstrated against the injustice and illegality of
one Governor superseding the grants of another; that the change
of jurisdiction could not alter the state of private property; that
the object of the Crown was originally to give the lands to the settlers; and finally, that it made no difference to the King which province held the jurisdiction if the quit-rents were not to be changed
from their New Hampshire establishment of nine-pence sterling the
hundred acres, though the Grants under the colony of New York
established them at two shillings and six pence. Those just and
equitable assertions weighed not with the Governor and Council
of New York so much as the fees, and they determined to persevere in re-granting the lands, and to enforce obedience to their
measures both by civil and military law. The Governor used
however some policy to complete his injustice, he made a difference between the settlers on the east and west sides of the Green
Mountains. Some leading characters on the east side, by yielding
up their New Hampshire grants, had new or confirmation grants
from

from New York on paying half fees.*   This plan was intended to
divide the people, while the settlers on the west side had their
lands re-granted, and were called on to acknowledge themselves
tenants to the Grantees under New York; this demand was not
21 complied with by the settlers, who replied that the fee simple
of the lands rested in the possessors.   The settlers called a
Convention of Representatives from the several towns on the west
side of the Green Mountains, who, on mature deliberation, agreed
to send an Agent to the Court of Great Britain, to state to the
King and Council the illegal and unjust proceedings of the Governor of New York, and to obtain redress of their grievance ;
they appointed Samuel Robinson, Esq; of Bennington, as their
Agent ; he accordingly repaired to London, and stated the grievance that the people laboured under, through the illegal conduct
of the Governor and Council of New York, but unfortunately was
taken sick and died, and was buried in Westminster-Abbey.   After his death, his Majesty and Privy Council took the Petition
into consideration ; and in July, 1767, passed an order, " His
" Majesty doth hereby strictly charge, require, and command, that
" the Governor or Commander in Chief of his Majesty's province
" of New York, for the time being, do not, upon pain of his Ma-
" jesty's highest displeasure, presume to make any grants whatso-
" ever, of any part of the lands described in the said report, until
" his Majesty's further pleasure shall be known concerning the
" same."[1]   This Royal prohibition was sent to the Governor, but
was kept private by him and his Council, for near two years.   In
the mean time the persecutions of the settlers were carried on by
the Governor and his land-monopolists.   About this time Smith's
22 History of New York was industriously circulated, in which
he attempts to prove that the colony had an ancient and in-
disputable title to the lands west of Connecticut river, in virtue of
a grant of King Charles II. to his brother James Duke of York,
containing " all the lands from the west side of Connecticut river,
" to the east side of Delaware-bay."

* The fees to the Governor of New Hampshire, for granting a township, were about three hundred Dollars ; under the Governor of New
York they generally exceeded two thousand Dollars.

---

[1] [Mr. Allen is in error in regard to Mr. Robinson. His death did
not take place till October, 27, 1767, more than three months after the
prohibitory order was made. He was interred in the burial ground belonging to the Rev. Mr. Whitefield's Church. For an account of his
mission and death, see *H. Hall's Vt.*, chap. IX, p. 85–97.]

In order to promote a further division between the people on the east and west side of the Green Mountains, the Governor of New York gave civil and military commissions to the leading characters on the east side.   Mr. Nathan Stone, of Windsor, raised a large party to oppose the overbearing power of the Governor and Council of New York, but finally was overpowered and submitted ; and soon after was appointed Colonel of the militia in the county of Cumberland, which then included all the New Hampshire grants east of the Green Mountains and west of Connecticut river.   This county being so extensive, and other men wishing for preferment, the Governor and Council divided it, and established the county of Gloucester to the north.   The new county was divided into half shires, Newbury and Kingsland,* and (strange to relate) a *log* Court House and Goal were erected at the latter place, though in the wilderness, and eight miles distant from any settlement ; there the Courts were opened and adjourned to Newbury.   The Governor, by this stratagem, partially brought the eastern counties to coincide with the interest of New York, and placed the western district in the interior of the Government, thereby thinking to compel them to submit as tenants to the Grantees, under New York ; forgetting that men, who had braved every danger and hardship attending the settlement of an uncultivated country, would not tamely submit to a mercenary Governor and a set of land-jobbers, having no legal or equitable right to the land and labours of others ; the contest grew warm and serious ; writs of ejectment were issued, and served on sundry persons, and returned to the supreme Court at Albany ; some officers were opposed by the people and prevented serving their writs.

Ethan Allen, Esq ; a proprietor under the New Hampshire Grants, was appointed by the people their Agent ; his first step was to wait on the Governor of New Hampshire, and obtain copies of the Royal orders and instructions, on which his Excellency had granted and given patents of lands in the western part of the province of New Hampshire ; with these copies and the original charters or grants, he waited on Mr. Ingersoll, an eminent barrister of Connecticut, who accompanied him to Albany, to defend the settlers under New Hampshire Grants, before the supreme Court, against the writs of ejectment.   When the first cause was brought before the Court, Mr. Ingersoll answered for the Defendant, and pleaded in bar to the action, and supported his plea by the Royal orders and instructions to Governor

* Now Washington.

Wentworth

Wentworth to make grants of lands in the province of New Hampshire, to such people as would settle upon and cultivate them ; and
also produced the grant and charter to the settlers, but the Judge
would not admit of their being received in Court as evidence, on
which Mr. Ingersoll saw the cause was already prejudged, and
did not attempt to defend it ; and judgment was rendered against
the Defendant.   Thus a precedent was established to annihilate
all the titles of land held under New Hampshire Grants,
west of Connecticut river.   Mr. Ingersoll and Mr. Allen retired from the Court, and in the evening Messrs. Kemp, Ban-
yar, and Duane, lawyers and land speculators of New York,
called on Mr. Allen, and among other conversation, Mr. Kemp,
the King's attorney, observed to Mr. Allen, *that the people
settled on the New Hampshire Grants should be advised to
make the best terms possible with their landlords, for might
often prevailed against right :* Mr. Allen answered, *The Gods of
the valleys are not Gods of the hills ;* Mr. Kemp asked for an ex-
planation, Mr. Allen replied, *that if he would accompany him to
Bennington, the phrase should be explained.*   Mr. Kemp proposed
to give Mr. Allen and other men of influence on the New Hampshire Grants, some large tracts of land, to secure peace and harmony, and the friendship of the leading men ; but the proposal
was rejected, and their conversation ended.[1]

25   On the return of Mr. Allen to Bennington, a convention of
the people met, and passed a resolution to support their
rights and property under the New Hampshire Grants, against
the usurpation and unjust claims of the Governor and Council of
New York, *by force,* as law and justice were denied them, and not
being able to stand in their Courts, before the intrigues and power
of a junto of New York land-jobbers, who controlled the civil
powers of the colony.

This was a bold stroke of a hundred men, who united to oppose
the most favoured colony under the Crown, and whose wealth and
numbers were great ; but the people on the grants rightly considered their controversy was not with the great body of the people ;
only with the Governor and Council of New York, and their land
associates, who were but a small and jesuitical part of the com
munity.

This distinction was kept up during the whole dispute in all the
publications against the tyranny and injustice of the rulers of New

---

[1] [These trials took place in June, 1770.]

York

York, which made friends abroad, and united the people at home, and greatly promoted migrations from New England.

Some Patents which began in New York on perambulating and re-measuring their lines, were extended into the towns of Pownal, Bennington, Shaftsbury, &c. about three miles on their western parts.

26 These claims were violently insisted upon (especially at Walloomscoick), and were as forcibly defended by the people, who determined to dispute every inch of ground which had been granted to them by the Governor of New Hampshire.

Civil officers from New York were therefore opposed by the people of New Hampshire Grants, who, in return, were indicted for riots, by the people of New York, from whence writs were issued, and their Sheriffs' officers sent to apprehend the delinquents. These officers were seized by the people, and severely chastised *with twigs of the Wilderness;* every day produced new events, which induced the settlers on the Grants to form themselves into a military association. Mr. Ethan Allen was appointed Colonel Commandant, and Messrs. Seth Warner, Remember Baker, Robert Cockran, Gideon Warren, and some others, were appointed Captains ; Committees of Safety were likewise appointed in the several towns west of the Green Mountains; though by order of the Governor of New York the south part of the Grants were annexed to the County of Albany, and the North formed into a County by the name of Charlotte, which extended some distance west of the district of the New Hampshire Grants. Here Justices of the Peace and Civil Courts were also appointed, and allowed (by the people) to act, when the title of Lands was not concerned, nor riots, nor sending people off the Grants without the concurrence of the Committee of Safety. The Governor of New
27 York had threatened to drive the military (his opposers) into the Green Mountains, from which circumstance they took the name of *Green Mountain Boys.* In consequence hereof the Convention passed a resolution that no officer from New York be allowed to carry out of the district of New Hampshire Grants, any person, without permission of the Committees of Safety ; or of the military Commanders. Surveyors of land under New York were forbid to run any lines within the Grants ; transgressors in this point were to be punished according to the judgment of a Court formed from among the elders of the people, or military commanders. Their punishment sometimes consisted in whipping severely with beech twigs, and banishment,
not

not to return on pain of suffering the *resentment* of the *Green Mountain Boys*. Mr. Hugh Monroe, an old offender, was taken, tried and ordered to be whipped on his naked back; he was tied to a tree and flogged till he fainted; on recovering he was whipped again until he fainted; he recovered and underwent a third lashing until he fainted; his wounds were then dressed, and he was banished the district of the New Hampshire Grants. These severities were used to deter people from endangering their lives, and to prevent aid being given to the land claimants of New York; they proved to answer the purpose, and the *Green Mountain Boys* soon became the terror of their adversaries. When the Sheriffs' officers came to collect debts they were used with civility, and the cause of the people was explained; in this way the strength of the enemy was weakened, and the cause of the settlers gained strength and credit.

Colonel Reed, a British officer, had obtained from the Governor of New York a grant of lands that covered most part of the townships of New Haven, Ferrisburgh, and Panton; he went and took possession of a saw mill by force, at the lower falls on Otter Creek, with a quantity of logs and boards, and refused to permit (the Pangborns) the owners and builders to make use of any part of their property. The Colonel kept possession and built a corn-mill, sundry houses, and settled some Scotch families on the premises. Several riots happened in consequence of opposing surveyors and civil officers under the authority of New York.

The Convention met again, and passed a *decree* forbidding all persons taking grants or confirmation of grants under the Governor of New York. This decree tended to unite very much the settlers in the common cause. About the same time the Legislature of New York passed an act authorizing the Sheriffs of Albany and Charlotte counties to call out the *posse comitatus* in case they should be opposed in the execution of their office, and if any person refused to obey the order of the Sheriff, he was subject to a fine of 75 dollars and six months imprisonment. The Governor of New York issued his proclamation, offering a reward of 150 pounds for Colonel Ethan Allen, and 50 pounds each for Warner and five others therein named, to any person that should take and confine them in any gaol in the colony of New York. Allen and the other proscribed persons issued another proclamation, offering five pounds to any person who should take and deliver *John Taber Kemp*, Esq; Attorney General of the colony of New York, to any officer in the militia of the Green Mountain

tain Boys, and published the same in the public newspapers in New England.[1]

The supreme Court at Albany having awarded a judgment on a writ of ejectment against James Brackenridge, of Bennington, Esq. the Sheriff of the County of Albany summoned the *posse comitatus* to go with him and assist him in putting the Plaintiff in possession of the Defendant's house and lands. Accordingly 750 men well armed followed the Sheriff. The news of the Sheriff's approach with an armed force so formidable, was a trial of the courage and independent spirit of the Green Mountain Boys, who, under every discouragement, except that of being in the wrong, had determined on justice or death. The settlers in general were poor and widely spread, which made it difficult to convene them in a body sufficient to encounter 750 men; in this case they had to oppose the most favorite colony under the Crown, whose population was large, the land monopolists rich; the Governor and Council intriguing, and who had, by contending with Connecticut and New Jersey, in the settlement of boundary lines, gained considerably, and also laid claim to the western part of Massachusett's bay. Notwithstanding these discouraging circumstances, the officers of the Green Mountain Boys collected as many men as they could, (being only about three hundred) who arrived at the house of Mr. Brackenridge some hours before the Sheriff; they were formed into three divisions; the house was prepared, and an officer with 18 men put in it for defence; about 120 were placed in a wood, behind trees, near the road, through which the Sheriff must march, and would naturally halt his men while he went to demand possession of the premises; the other division was stationed behind a ridge of land in a meadow, within gun-shot of the house, and out of sight of the Sheriff's men. Thus the ambuscade was formed to have a cross fire on the Sheriff's without endangering themselves, and to be ready against the Sheriff forced the door, which was to be known by hoisting a red flag above the top of the chimney. When the Sheriff approached all were silent; he and his men were compleatly within the ambuscade, before they discovered their situation; Mr. Ten Eyck, the Sheriff, went to the house and demanded entrance as Sheriff of the County of Albany, and threatened on refusal, to force the door; the answer was, "attempt it, and you are a dead man." He repeated his demand and threat, without

---

[1] [Governor Tryon's proclamation was dated December 9, 1771, and that of Allen, Baker and Cochran, the 5th of February following; see *H. Hall's Vt.*, p. 134.]

using

using any force ; and received for a second answer, *hideous groans
from those within!* At this time the two divisions exhibited
their hats on the points of their guns, which appeared to be
31

more numerous than they really were. The Sheriff and his posse
seeing their dangerous situation, *and not being interested in the
dispute,* made a hasty retreat, so that a musket was not fired on
either side ; which gave satisfaction to and cemented the union of
the inhabitants, and raised their consequence in the neighboring
colonies.[1] Riots and disputes continued to increase, and many
transgressors from New York underwent the discipline of the
whip: Mr. J. Monroe, who had acted as a justice of the peace
under New York, had rendered himself obnoxious by his partiali-
ty for New York, and persecution of the settlers of the grants.
Colonel Allen, with a party, went to his house very early one
morning, and fired several shot into the upper part of it, which
alarmed him to such a degree that he fled to New York.

About this time a banditti came to Arlington, wounded and
took prisoner Captain Remember Baker, (one of the seven proscribed persons) and his wife was also severely wounded with a
sword. They put Baker into a sleigh, and drove off with great
speed for Albany. An express was sent to Bennington with the
tidings ; instantly on the news, ten men mounted their horses and
pursued them near thirty miles, and intercepted the party at a
cross road, (about 50 men) on full speed. This banditti thought
the ten horsemen were an advanced guard of a larger party,
32
and therefore left their prisoner and fled. Captain Baker being nearly exhausted by loss of blood, was taken care of, his
wounds dressed, and then carried home to his wife and children,
to their no small joy, and that of the Green Mountain Boys.[2]

Information reached Bennington, that Governor Tryon was on
his way by water to Albany, with British troops, in order to subject or destroy the Green Mountain Boys: This news was readily credited, as the royal troops had been lately used on Bateman's
Patent, in the colony of New York, to quell some disputes about
the titles or rents of lands ; and it was known that the subsequent
Grantees of the New Hampshire Grants had applied to the Governor of New York for a similar favour. New and more serious
troubles daily appeared. The Committees of Safety met the military officers to consult on measures proper to be taken. They
found matters had come to a crisis that compelled them either to

[1] [The posse were at Mr. Breakenridge's, July 19, 1771.]
[2] [The capture and rescue of Baker took place March 21, 1772.]
submit

submit and become tenants to the land jobbers of New York, or to take the field against a royal Governor and British troops ; either step seemed like the forlorn hope. Having reflected on the justice of their cause, the hardships, expence of money, and labour they had been at in building and cultivation, they, therefore, unanimously resolved, *that it was their duty to oppose Governor*
33   *Tryon and his troops to the utmost of their power ;* (and thereby convince him and his council, that they were punishable by the Green Mountain Boys) *for disobeying his Majesty's prohibitory orders, of July,* 1767. The plan of defensive operation was the next question in case of an attack. The elders of the people urged the propriety of sending a flag to the Governor, to enquire whether an accommodation was impracticable ? the military objected and said, that step would shew pusilanimity as well as confidence in the Governor, who had proved himself at North Carolina *to be not worthy of confidence ;* and besides, no officer could be found to be bearer of a flag to him.* The elders of the people assured the military officers that they would afford them every degree of assistance in their power, advising them to concert among themselves the plans of defence, and then retired.†
34   The military sent a person to Albany, who had not been indicted as a rioter, to see the Governor and some of his principal officers, so as to know them again ; to discover their strength, and order of marching ; and when they would leave Albany. Having performed this business he had orders to return and join six other good marksmen, and station themselves at a certain place in a wood near the road that the enemy were to march ; the Governor was to be pointed out, and the expert marksmen were to fire, one by one at him, until he fell from his horse, then to give an Indian *whoop* and raise their ambuscade ; and should the enemy afterwards continue their march, they were to return to the

* Except Captain Stephen Fay.
† Mr. Tryon, while Governor of North Carolina, called in the military to quell some disturbances among the people called Regulators. On the approach of the two parties the Regulators sent a flag to the Governor ; it was received, and an answer was wrote, signed, and delivered to the officer of the flag, and he departed with it. The *Aid-de-Camp* of the Governor suggested a clause to be added, which the Governor approved of ; the officer of the flag was ordered to return and deliver up the letter; he refused to obey the order, and said he had brought a message and delivered it, and had an answer given to deliver, which he would deliver according as directed.—On that answer the Governor ordered his men to fire on the officer of the flag ; they fired and killed him, by which means they obtained the answer.

road

road at a fixed place, and take down two or three more of the
chief officers; then to hasten and join the main body, who were to
be prepared to receive Governor Tryon's troops, and to decide
the fate of the inhabitants of the New Hampshire Grants.

The messenger, on his return from Albany, made the following
report, *that the British troops were wind bound some miles below
Albany, and were destined to relieve the garrisons of Oswego,
Niagara and Detroit; and Governor Tryon was not with them;*
of course the preparations for a battle were suspended. The
Governor and his land-jobbers soon got information of this preparation; and they were both intimidated and convinced, that the
Green Mountain Boys would fight even the King's troops if sent
35 to decide the titles of land, and to dispossess the inhabitants
who rescued them out of a state of nature. This alarm answered every purpose that a victory possibly could have done,
without shedding blood. [1]

The Convention met and passed a decree, forbidding all inhabitants in the district of the New Hampshire Grants, *to hold, take,
or accept any office of honour or profit under the colony of New
York,* and all civil and military officers who had acted under authority of the Governor or Legislature of New York, were required to suspend their functions on pain of being *viewed.* This
decree united the people in the common cause, and induced many
in New England to move and settle on the New Hampshire Grants.
Mr. J. Monroe, whose house had been fired at, met Captain Warner and Mr. Sherwood, when some provoking words passed, and
Warner drew his sword and smote Monroe on his head, but his
thick hat, hair, and skull saved his brains, and broke Warner's
sword.

Colonel Allen, with a party of men, thought it high time to pay
a visit to the plantation and mills which Colonel Reed had taken
possession of in New-haven as aforesaid; he gave Colonel Reed's
tenants a short time to remove their goods, and then burnt the
houses, ordering the tenants to quit the district, unless they took
or purchased under the New Hampshire Grants.

36 Colonel Allen went then to Colonel Reed's corn mill; but
found it could not be burnt separately from Pangborn's saw-
mill; he ordered the mill-stones to be broken and thrown down

---

[1] [This alarm from an apprehended military attack upon the settlers
was in April, 1772. See *Doc. His. N. Y.*, Vol. IV, p. 778.]

the

the falls, and the roof taken off, and put Pangborns in possession
of their property; assuring the people that henceforth all who
held titles under the grants of New Hampshire, should be protected against the lawless invaders from New York.

The Sheriff of Charlotte county attempted to arrest Captain
Cockran for riots and outrages, who was too well armed for a
civil officer, and the Sheriff, for safety, made the best of his way
out of the territory of the Green Mountain Boys.

The first settlers of Clarendon, held under an absolute title of
Colonel Henry H. Lydius, who pretended to have a title from
Governor Pownal, of Massachusett's, but it was no more than an
order of location, beginning at the mouth of Otter Creek, thence
extending 60 miles up the Creek, and its width 20 miles; a part
of these lands had been granted by the Governor of New York to
James Duane, and others, under the name of Socialboro'. The
settlers were in favour of New York, and pretended to hold under
Lydius; they, therefore, declined purchasing under New Hampshire or New York, until the dispute should be settled. Disturbances had frequently sprung up in this place; Mr. Spencer, an
artful, intriguing, and designing man, acted as a justice of the
37 peace under New York, and often sent writs against the inhabitants of that and other places. Colonel Allen, with near
a hundred men, set off for Clarendon, to terrify and frighten
Spencer out of the country. Information of the intended visit
reached Spencer, and he fled into the woods. Allen and his party
went to his house, but he could not be found. After scouting the
woods in vain, they marched three miles, and put up for the night.
Towards day-light Allen, with ten men, went again to Spencer's
house, and, with a log, forced the door, then with swords and
pistols rushed in, crying out for Spencer to appear, but he had not
ventured to return home. They left the house and joined their
party, where a small dog was discovered, whose name was *Tryon;*
they took and cut the poor animal in pieces with their swords, for
no other cause than that of being called Tryon; they held up the
different parts of the dog, and vociferated, *Thus will we do unto
Tryon.* Mr. Spencer was so much alarmed at this visit to his
house, and the fate of the dog, that he fled to New York, and
matters remained quiet for a time.

In the spring of 1772, Governor Tryon addressed a letter to
the Rev. Mr. Dewey, of Bennington, which held out a glimmering
hope of pacification. The Governor requested Mr. Dewey to interpose his good offices, and state the grievances of the people,
assuring

assuring him that they should be redressed so far as was consistent, and that if the people chose to send agents to negociate an accommodation, they should be received and protected, excepting Mr. Ethan Allen, Seth Warner, Remember Baker, and Robert Cockran. This invitation was kindly accepted, and Captain Stephen Fay, with Dr. Jonas Fay, were appointed agents of the settlers on the grants to go to New York, for an adjustment of the claims of the grantees under New Hampshire. Accordingly the agents waited upon and laid before the Governor and Council of New York all matters of grievance, and a suspension of all crown actions against the settlers on the grants took place in consequence, until his Majesty's will and pleasure should be further known: and further it was recommended by the Governor and Council to the land claimants under New York, to put a stop, during this period, to all respecting titles of land suits. The agents found that nothing could be done effectually with the Governor and Council to secure the interest of the settlers; therefore, after having put the business in a train of negociation, they took leave and returned to their constituents. Their reports gave union and strength to the settlers, and proved a sufficient caution against the collusions of New York. Sundry letters afterwards passed between Governor Tryon and Mr. Dewey on this subject, which had a tendency to keep matters quiet a little while. During this seeming friendly correspondence, the land jobbers of New York privately sent Mr. Cockborn, a surveyor, to make further locations within the district of the New Hampshire grants; some knowledge of this transpiring, pains were taken to find him out. At length Ira Allen discovered his destination, by traversing the wilderness, and Captain Warner and Baker, with a number of men, went in the pursuit; they found and took him in Bolton, near one hundred and thirty miles north of Bennington: great part of this way was in the Wilderness. They broke and destroyed his instruments, and tried him by a court martial; he was found guilty, and banished the district of the grants, on pain of death if he ever returned. The correspondence then going on between the Governor and the people for the restoration of peace and friendship, saved Mr. Cockburn a severe whipping.

In the autumn Lieutenant Ira Allen being desirous of exploring the northern part of the district, for settlement, was accompanied by Captain Baker and five men, who went from Skeensborough-falls by water to the lower falls in Onion River, where they discovered and took a boat and some provisions, with two men, one of whom informed Allen and Baker that they were with a surveying party from

from New York under Captain Stephens, who had with him five men and three guns. Baker and his party had only one gun, a case of pistols, and a cutlass. It was concluded to await their return, as hunger would soon force them in ; therefore, at evening, 40 they stationed a sentinel, secured their prisoners, and went to rest. Next morning, about sun-rise, two boats were seen coming towards the *camp*, with six white men and thirteen Indians, armed. Stephens and his five men landed, and the Indians were about to follow. Allen and Baker had one man who spoke the Indian language ; he told the Indians that " this was a land dispute between white men, and did not concern the Indians, who might hunt and fish wherever they pleased." At this the Indians went off, and left Stephens and his men prisoners.

They were released without any trial, or corporal punishment (on account of the subsisting negociations) and they promised not to return again. Baker, Allen, and the party went on, and explored the country, surveyed the township of Mansfield, and returned to the river in Bolton. Allen wishing further to explore the country, Captain Baker and one man returned with the boat to Skeensborough, and he and the four men remained, and traversed the wilderness. Being almost destitute of provisions, in consequence of a disappointment, they concluded to make the best of their way to Pitsford, nearly seventy miles through a wilderness. After travelling four days through the woods, brooks, and rivers, and over the range of Green Mountains, with only one dinner and three partridges for five men, they reached Pitsford, almost overcome with hunger and weakness. They were fed with 41 a crust of bread, then with pudding for an hour, then with a small piece of mutton and turnips. One man eat a double share, and soon fell asleep ; he was rolled over and over, and carried about for an hour, before they could awake him ; had they neglected him during that hour, he would have never awoke again : This should caution men not to eat too much after long abstinence, and when hunger has changed to faintness.

The agents of Colonel Reed found means (by hooping) to repair the stones of the corn-mill, and by that means kept possession. Mr. Allen, with one man, on passing that way, stopped at the mill, and caused the miller to break the stones into small pieces with a sledge, and throw them down the falls, and gave orders not to repair the mill again, on pain of suffering the *displeasure* of the Green Mountain Boys.

The

The Governor and his coadjutors seeing they could not make settlements, or get possession of the lands in the district of the grants, and that time and persecution had added strength and courage to the people, cunningly adopted another plan, by encouraging a number of Scotch emigrants to settle at New Haven falls, under the New York proprietors. Information of this was sent to Colonel Allen; whereupon he, with a number of men, repaired to New Haven falls, and built a block fort, but before it was finished, 42 some agents from the Scotch emigrants came from New York to view the country, and learn the nature of the dispute, prior to the removal of their families. Having discovered the nature of the different claims, they informed Col. Allen that they had been deceived, and that they had not migrated to settle on lands whose titles were contested, especially where garrisons were building to support them. Those emigrant strangers quitted the district of the grants, and afterwards settled on the Mohock River.

The families of Allen and Baker, with a view to guard the coasts against settlers under the grants of New York, erected another block fort at Colchester, near Onion River lower falls, with thirty-two port holes in the upper story, and well furnished with arms and ammunition.

A road was cut by these families, extending from Castleton to Colchester, being about seventy miles, which, with the forts now completed, contributed to facilitate the settlement of the northern part of the grants, and discouraged settlements under the claims of the New York patentees.

At Shelburne a few families had settled under the New York claimants, and these were permitted to remain so long as they continued peaceable, with leave to use their option as to purchasing under the New Hampshire titles.

43 The plan of the land monopolizers of New York was to get in possession and to occupy the lands contiguous to Champlain, as they had done on the east part of the grants adjoining Connecticut River, and thereby be able to subject the interior country. At this time New York was contending with Massachusett's, and claimed jurisdiction over the county of Berkshire, that lay east of the twenty miles line from Hudson's River, which was, in 1763, the established eastern boundary of New York, and so remains. Though the New Yorkers, to change that line, and establish *a precedent*, sent warrants into that county, in the jurisdiction

tion of Massachusett's, and took Joseph Bills and Gillom Belcher at Sandersfield, for (*the supposed to be*) forgers of New York paper currency, carried them to Albany, tried, condemned, and executed them, for a crime which (if committed) was committed twenty-five miles east of the jurisdiction of New York.

One evening Colonel Allen and Mr. Eli Roberts went into the house of Mr. Richardson at Bridport, and unexpectedly met with two serjeants and ten men from the garrison of Crown Point, well armed. The serjeants knew him; the soldiers were at the door, and before Allen saw his danger, it was too late to retreat. Thus situated, Allen called for liquor, and made merry with the serjeants, who observed that he and Roberts had each a gun and a case of pistols. They supped, and Allen and Roberts asked to be accommodated with beds, but were answered, that all were engaged by the serjeants. They then concluded to sleep in the barn, though the serjeants politely offered to give up one bed to them, which was not accepted, as the season was warm, and they well knowing that, for sake of the Governer's reward, the serjeants would endeavor to secure them. At bed time they were shewn to the barn, and, to blind suspicion, left their guns in the house; the serjeants saw them to the barn, and wished them good night. Soon as possible Miss Richardson brought them their guns, and they departed. The serjeants waited in the house till they supposed Allen and Roberts were asleep, then surrounded the barn, and sought in vain for their expected prey.

Mr. Hough, of Clarendon, by persuasion of the Governor of New York, had the imprudence to accept the office of a justice of the peace, under the jurisdiction of that colony, and was hardy enough to officiate as such; whereupon he was taken, and brought before the Committee of Safety at Sunderland, before whom he justified his conduct, and pleaded the jurisdiction of the colony of New York. The Committee ordered the resolution of the Convention of the New Hampshire grants to be read, *which forbid all persons holding any office, civil or military, under the colony of New York, within the said district.*

In the presence of a large concourse of people, the following judgment was pronounced, *that the prisoner be taken from the bar of this Committee of Safety, and tied to a tree, and there, on his naked back, to receive two hundred stripes; his back being*

being dressed, he should depart out of the district, and, on return, to suffer death, unless by special leave of Convention.[1]

This sentence was executed in a severe manner. He asked for and received a copy of his sentence, which, together with the receipt on his back, would, no doubt, be admitted as legal evidence before the Supreme Court and Governor of New York, though the King's warrant to Governor Wentworth, and his Excellency's sign manuel, with the great seal of the province of New Hampshire, were not.

In the summer of 1773, Mr. Ira Allen, with three men, went from the block fort on Onion River, in pursuit of a Mr. S. Gale, who, with a number of men, were surveying in the district of the New Hampshire grants, for the land jobbers of New York. Allen and his party traversed the district from east to west, through the townships of Waterbury, Middlesex, and Kingsland, to Moretown, alias Bradford, and Haverhill; and, at length, obtaining information of the surveyor's destination, they procured provisions and some spirits, and went again in quest of him; they discovered his line, and, by that, followed him to near the north east corner of the present town of Montpellier; here it ended, and he could not be traced further, because being apprised of his danger, he made a corner on dry land, and thus precipitately escaped, and Allen came to the corner an hour after he fled. On the sixteenth day they reached the block fort whence they sat out.

46

Dr. Samuel Adams, of Arlington, became friendly to the interterests of the monopolists of New York, and often spoke disrespectful of the Convention and system of the Green Mountain Boys, advising people to purchase lands under the New York titles. Such conversation tended to divide the people, and strengthen the enemy, who were much alarmed at the perseverance and summary mode made use of by the Green Mountain Boys, in punishing the claimants under, or partizans of New York, many of whom had been whipped almost to death. Therefore the New York grantees would have been willing to have sold their subsequent grants to the most influential characters, to cover their lands and improvements, in order to obtain peaceably the lands granted by New Hampshire, which were not settled, as well as that part

---

[1] [Hough had not only served as magistrate, but had been very active in procuring from the New York Assembly the passage of the outlawry act against Allen and others. His trial and punishment took place at Sunderland, January 30, 1775.]

of

of the country which had not been granted, considering themselves safe, and in the quiet possession of all the lands to the east of the Green Mountains.   Under these circumstances Doctor Adams was requested to change his conversation on the subject, or, at least, to be silent.,   The Doctor persisted, and declared that he would speak his mind, and converse as he pleased.   He also armed
47 himself with a pair of good pistols and other private weapons, and gave out that he would *silence* any man who attempted to molest him.   However, the Doctor was soon taken by surprize, and carried to the Green Mountain tavern, at Bennington, where the Committee heard his defence, and then ordered him to be tied in an armed chair, and hoisted up to the sign (*a cat-a-mount's skin stuffed, sitting upon the sign-post, 25 feet from the ground, with large teeth, looking and grinning towards New York*) and there to hang two hours, in sight of the people, as a punishment merited by his enmity to the rights and liberty of the inhabitants of the New Hampshire grants.   The judgment was executed, to the no small merriment of a large concourse of people.   The Doctor was let down and dismissed by the Committee, with an admonition to go and sin no more.   This mild and exemplary disgrace had a salutary effect on the Doctor, and many others.

About this time the Convention of the said district of New Hampshire Grants appointed Messrs. James Breckenridge and Jehial Hawley, as their agents, to repair to London, and in the name and behalf of the said people, to prefer a memorial to his Majesty and Privy Council, for redress of the aforesaid grievances from the colony of New York, and to further negociate, in the
48 name and behalf of said people, as circumstances might require.

They repaired to London, made some progress in their mission, and favourable measures were taken ; but after considerable delays, the approaching American war seemed to bar any final decision, and they returned, without accomplishing the objects of their delegation.[1]

Colonel and Lieutenant Allen were on a visit at their brother Heman Allen's, at Salisbury in Connecticut, near the east line of the colony of New York.   A plot was laid by a number of people in the colony of New York to take Colonel Allen, and carry him to Poughkeepsie gaol, and thereby obtain the premium promised

---

[1] [Messrs. Breakenridge and Hawley sailed for England late in the fall of 1772. *Doc. His. N. Y.*, Vol. IV, p. 802.]

by Governor Tryon.   One Robert M'Cormick, who had done business for Heman Allen, was appointed *the decoy duck* on this occasion.   His plan was to go and find which room Colonel Allen
slept in, then to inform the gang, who were well armed with
swords and pistols, and had two sleighs prepared.   At a proper
hour in the night, Mr. M'Cormick was to open the door, and conduct them to the Colonel's apartment, seize, force him into a
sleigh, and drive off with all speed out of Connecticut.   The plan
thus laid, M'Cormick parted with his *gang*, went to Heman Allen's
house, and was as usual kindly received, and offered a bed.   It
was observed by the family that M'Cormick was unusually reserved
in his conversation and drinking.   He made some feint en-
49 quiries about Colonel and Lieutenant Allen, who had rode
out that afternoon, but were expected to return every moment.
Heman Allen, from these circumstances, surmized some plot was
on foot against his brothers ; and, on the Colonel's return, informed
him of his suspicions.   Colonel Allen suddenly taxed M'Cormick
of being concerned : He confessed such a plot was in agitation,
and that he had come privately to apprise them of it.   M'Cormick departed, and told the gang what had happened, and they
thought it prudent to suspend their intentions.   The Colonel and
Lieutenant armed, however, for their defence, but were not dis-
turbed.   The spirit of opposition and resentment had arisen so
high in the course of these proceedings, that in March, 1774, the
Government of New York passed an act, the most mandatory and
despotic of any thing which ever appeared in the British colonies.
Among other extraordinary exertions of " vindictive power, it
contained,* " to the disgrace and shame of the authors and abet-
tors, this curious clause ; " and in case the said offenders shall
" not respectively surrender themselves pursuant to such orders
" of his Excellency the Governor, or of the Governor and Com-
" mander in Chief for the time being, to be made in Council as
" aforesaid ; he or they so neglecting or refusing to surrender
50 " himself, or themselves as aforesaid, [i. e. within the space
" of seventy days next after the first publication of the or-
" der] shall, from the day to be appointed for his or their sur-
" render as aforesaid, be adjudged, deemed, and (if indicted
" for a capital offence hereafter to be perpetrated) to be con-
" victed and attainted of felony, and shall suffer death, as in
" cases of persons convicted and attainted of felony by verdict
" and judgment, without benefit of clergy ; and that it shall and
" may be lawful to, and for the supreme court of judicature of
" this colony, or the courts of oyer and terminer, or general gaol

* *Williams's History of Vermont*, page 222.

delivery

" delivery, for the respective counties aforesaid, to award execu-
" tion against such offender or offenders, so indicted for a capital
" offence, perpetrated after the passing of this act, in such man-
" ner as if he or they had been convicted or attainted in the
" supreme courts of judicature, or before such courts of oyer and
" terminer, or general gaol delivery respectively." This act of
proscription caused a meeting of the committees of the several
towns on the west side of the Green Mountains, to convene in
Manchester, April, 1774, who came to the following resolve:
" That for the future, every necessary preparation be made, and
" that our inhabitants hold themselves in readiness, at a minute's
" warning, to aid and defend such friends of ours, who, for their
" merit and attachment to the great and general cause, are falsely
" denominated rioters; but that we will not act any thing, more
51 " or less, but on the defensive, and always encourage due ex-
" ecution of law, in civil cases, and also in criminal prose-
" cutions, *that are so indeed;* and that we will assist, to the utmost
" of our power, the officers appointed for that purpose."[1]

The proscribed military were more pointed and severe in an address directed to the people of the counties of Albany and Charlotte, and others who might be called on to assist the authority of
New York, in these words: that " we will kill and destroy any
persons, whomsoever, that shall presume to be accessory, aiding
or assisting, in taking any of us." This, with the preceding resolution, was published in newspapers and hand-bills, to deter any
person from carrying the said acts into execution, and to prevent
the effusion of blood. In this, the inhabitants of said district conceived that they were only contending for justice, as rigidly as it
was forcibly and illegally debarred them by the Governor and
Council of New York.[2]

At this Convention, a printed constitution, or more properly
rules for the future government of the district of the grants were
published, as a general defence became necessary to guard against
the usurpations of the colony of New York.

After the accession of King William III. the first commission
issued was, to appoint Colonel Henry Sloughter *Governor of the*
52 *colony of New York, and the territories thereon depending in*
America. The colony of *New York* did not, however, ex-

---

[1] [For this extraordinary act of outlawry in full, see *Slade's Vt. State*
Papers, p. 42–48.]

[2] [*Slade's State Papers*, p. 49–54.]

tend

tend to Albany ; but that country, and the remainder now claimed
by the Governor of New York, were territorial jurisdictions, con-
tinuing still *in residuum*, under authority of the crown.　The same
forms have since been observed in commissions to the Governors
of New York, until the independence of America.

In 1773, Colonel Allen made a collection of documents respecting grants to the Plymouth Company, Sir John Young and others,
Lord Say and Sele, of the settlement of the boundary line between
the provinces of Massachusett's and New Hampshire, the grant to
the Duke of York, and the history of the first settlement of New
Amsterdam, now New York.

From these documents, and the oppressions exercised by the
Governor and Council of New York, Colonel Allen wrote and
published a book of nearly 400 pages, in 1774.　By this book and
others, the cause of the people became of public notoriety through
the colonies, as the newspapers were in every part circulating
these proceedings, which sowered the minds of the people much
against the British Government, as it was generally supposed that
the Governor and Council of New York were countenanced by Government ; and one circumstance which contributed to this idea,
53 was the difference in quit-rents, annually payable to the crown
under New Hampshire ; they were ninepence sterling on each
hundred acres of land ; in New York proposed Grants they would
be two shillings and sixpence sterling per hundred acres ; these
measures contributed much towards hastening and bringing about
the revolution of America ; the consequence the Green Mountain
Boys had acquired abroad, through those violent struggles, to preserve their property in the first instance, and then to protect themselves against the tyranny of the late colony of New York, will, in
some measure, appear from Colonel Ethan Allen's being applied to
immediately after the battle at Lexington, both by the Governor
and Council of Connecticut, and a board of war at Water Town,
near Boston, to take Ticonderoga, Crown Point, &c.

Hence, in the year 1774, to get rid of the colony of New York,
a plan was formed by Colonel Allen, Mr. Amos Bird, and other
principal characters among the people, in conjunction with Colonel Philip Skene, to have established a new royal colony, which
was to contain the grants of New Hampshire, west of Connecticut
River, and the country north of the Mohawk River, to latitude 45°
north, and bounded west by Iroquois River and Lake Ontario.
　　　　　　　　　　　　　　　　　　　　　　　　　　Colonel

Colonel Skene had been an officer in his Majesty's service, and had retired on a large patent of land lying at the south end of Lake 54 Champlain, which was called Skenesboro'*, a proper scite for the capital of the new colony, of which he was proposed to be Governor.

The honor and lucrative prospects thus presented to Colonel Skene, stimulated him to go to London at his own expence, to solicit the accomplishment of an important object to individuals, and to the public: for had he succeeded, the people who had settled under the royal grants of New Hampshire would have been quiet, and relieved from the oppressive conduct of the Governor and Council of the colony of New York.

Colonel Skene's first object, after his arrival in London, was to get himself appointed Governor of the garrisons of Ticonderoga and Crown Point, which being effected, his friends advised him that, to obtain the grand object in view, he should bring forward a petition from the people on the premises to the King and Privy Council, stating, that in order to restore harmony in the said district, and for the convenience of administering justice in a department very remote and extensive, his Majesty would be pleased to establish the territory aforesaid, with colonial privileges, and appoint Colonel Philip Skene Governor thereof.

55 Information of these matters was transmitted from London to the people of the said district; but the calamity of an approaching war in America put an end to the proposed negociation for a royal colony, that was to surround that important water Lake Champlain.

The disputes between Great Britain and the American colonies had arose to such an height, that a congress convened in Philadelphia, September 5th, 1774, and recommended to the people to maintain their liberties in such ways as might be found necessary. In consequence all the courts of justice in the neighboring colonies, that were held under royal authority, were either shut up or adjourned, without doing business. In March, 1775, an attempt was made to hold a court of justice at Westminster, in the county of Cumberland, which was prevented by the people, who had early taken possession of the Court-house, and the Judges were refused entrance at the usual hour when the Courts were opened; therefore, they and the officers of the Court retired, until about

* Now Whitehall.

eleven

eleven o'clock at night, when they returned, and were again refused admittance ; whereupon they fired into the house, and killed
one man and wounded several.　This inflamed the minds of the
people to an high degree, who next day flocked from every part
of the county ; a coroner's inquest sat on the body, and brought
in a verdict that the man was *wilfully murdered by the Court party*,
some of whom they seized, and sent to Northampton gaol in
56　Massachusetts, but who were released on application to the
Chief Justice of New York.　The committees, exasperated at this
event, met at Westminster the following month, from a large number of towns, and came to the following resolutions : " That it is
" the duty of the inhabitants, wholly to renounce and resist the
" administration of the government of New York, until such time
" as the lives and property of the inhabitants may be secured by
" it, or until such time as they can have an opportunity to lay
" their grievances before His Most Gracious Majesty in council,
" together with a proper remonstrance against the unjustifiable
" conduct of that government ; with an humble petition to be
" taken out of so oppressive a jurisdiction, and either annexed to
" some other government, or erected and incorporated into a new
" one, as may appear best for the inhabitants."　The animosity
which subsisted between the two parties of New York, and the
New Hampshire grants, partially gave way before greater events,
which involved the colonies in a war of eight years, and terminated
in the acknowledgement of American independence.

The battle of Lexington, which happened on the 19th of April,
1775, threw the whole continent into a ferment, and preparations
were every where making for opposition to the unjust claims of
the British cabinet.　The Governor and Council of Connecticut
immediately sent Major Halsey and Noah Phelps, Esquires,
57　to the New Hampshire Grants, requesting Colonel Allen to
raise the Green Mountain Boys, and to go and take the garrisons
of Ticonderoga and Crown Point ; so consequential were the Vermonteers, that an application for offensive operations came at the
same time from different colonies.　Colonel Allen forthwith ad-
vertised his principal officers to meet him at Bennington, where
they met, and in a council of war it was resolved, that a secret
and forced march should be undertaken without delay against
those garrisons, in order to take them by surprize.　This measure
was necessary, as Ticonderoga was a strong and well fortified garrison, and well supplied with cannon, though not strongly manned
in time of peace.

Colonel

Colonel Allen had only small arms without bayonets ; he, by
the assistance of his officers, soon raised about 180 men, and having set guards on different roads, he marched and arrived with his
troops nearly opposite to Fort Ticondaroga, on the night between
the 7th and 8th of May, 1775 : There he was joined by Colonel
Benedict Arnold with only one man, who were sent by order of a
council of war from Water Town, near Boston, to Colonel Allen,
for the same purpose that Halsey and Phelps were from Connecticut. He produced his orders, and attempted to take the command, which Colonel Allen and his officers did not permit. At
length, after considerable altercation, Colonel Arnold was admit-
58 ted as second in command, and to enter the garrison with
Colonel Allen, *at his left hand.* All possible dispatch was
then made to cross the lake, about a mile in an oblique direction ;
they could find only very small boats : but with them, by passing
and repassing, they got over about 80 men by the dawn of day,
when Colonel Allen ordered an immediate attack on the garrison,
which consisted of nearly an equal number of men, as he apprehended danger of being discovered by the approaching morning
light, if he waited for the remainder of his men to join him. It
being a peacable time, a *wicket* gate was left open wide enough
for two men to pass a-breast ; when Colonels Allen and Arnold approached, the out sentinel attempted to fire, but his gun did not
go off ; he turned and run through the wicket gate, and Allen and
Arnold rushed in after him, and their men followed them. As
soon as they were within the garrison, Allen made a pass with
his sword at the sentinel, who defended himself with his musket,
but received a slight wound on his head. On this the assailants
made an hideous yell in imitation of the Indians, then demanded
an immediate surrender of the garrison. Captain De la Place,
Commandant of the garrison, appeared in his shirt at the head of
one pair of stairs, which were outside leading to the parade ;
there Colonel Allen met him. De la Place demanded to know by
what authority he (Colonel Allen) required the surrender of the
garrison ? Colonel Allen answered, *in the name of the Great Je-*
59 *hovah, and the Continental Congress !* The garrison was immediately surrendered, without firing a gun. The remainder
of Colonel Allen's men having crossed the lake, a party was sent
by water, as soon as possible, to Crown Point, under the command
of Captain Warner ; previous to this, Colonel Allen had sent orders to Captain Baker, of Onion River, forty miles north of Crown
Point, to come with his company and assist ; (and though be-
lated) yet he met and took two small boats on their way, to give
the alarm to Fort St. John. Captain Warner and Baker appeared
before Crown Point, nearly at the same time ; the garrison having
only

only few men surrendered without opposition.   In the mean time
Colonel Arnold, with the best water crafts that could be found,
proceeded with all possible speed, with a small detachment of men
to Fort St. John's, in order to take a sloop of war with 16 guns,
which he effected by surprize, and brought her away.

Colonel Allen having made proper regulations respecting the garrisons and prisoners at Ticondaroga, set off with 60 men for Fort
St. John's, and met Colonel Arnold with his prize ; he proceeded
on, and arrived there in the evening, and was informed that 150
British troops were on their way from Montreal, and would be at
St. John's by break of day.   This news induced Colonel Allen
and his officers to attempt to maintain their ground ; in the night
they formed an ambuscade for the party coming against them, but
60 he and his men having had no rest for three days and nights,
and being weighed down by fatigue and sleep, they raised the
ambush and crossed the lake, taking all the boats away with them.
Early next morning, Captain Amstruser arrived at St. John's, and
fired some Field-pieces, and shot at Colonel Allen's men, who answered with bullets from their muskets, then returned to Crown
Point and Ticondaroga, without having a man killed or much hurt.
Thus, in a few days, at the commencement of hostilities between
the British and the Americans, two hundred undisciplined men,
with small arms, without a single bayonet, made themselves masters of the garrisons of Ticondaroga, Crown Point, and St. Johns,
a sloop of war of 16 guns, about eighty prisoners, near 300 pieces
of cannon, shot, shells, &c. &c. so that the stone which the builders rejected, became the head of the corner, *to the honour of the
Green Mountain Boys.*   It is to be remembered, that this was the
first offensive part taken against Great Britain in the American
revolution.   Those troops of Colonel Allen kept possession of the
two former garrisons, until Colonel Benjamin Hinman's regiment
from Connecticut arrived, and by order of congress relieved them.
The prisoners were sent to Hartford in Connecticut.

In June, 1775, Mr. Brook Watson,* a British Merchant, with
two young noblesse of Canada, arrived at Crown Point with pass-
61 ports from the continental congress, directing the commanding
officer to give them a passage over the lake into Canada.
The officers and men belonging to Colonel Hinman's regiment
were not acquainted with the lake and country ; therefore, Lieutenant Ira Allen, and some Green Mountain Boys, undertook to
carry those gentlemen over the province line, to some settlements

* Late Lord Mayor of London.

in

in Lower Canada. Having almost reached the south line of Canada, Lieutenant Allen was convinced, in his own mind, that Mr. Watson (although he professed to be) was no friend to the American cause, notwithstanding his papers from the President of Congress, and his public and fair speeches at Crown Point; and apprehending danger from some Indians near the Canada line, (who might not understand or respect flags of truce) gave his men orders to new prime their guns, and to be ready for defence, at which Mr. Watson and the two Frenchmen objected, and attempted to seize their pistols to prevent obedience to the orders, but they were soon silenced, and let their pistols rest. Mr. Watson then requested to be put on shore at the nearest point of land, and both parties being willing to separate, the boat was ordered to shore accordingly, and Mr. Watson and the two Frenchmen were landed in a swamp three miles from any house, with instructions to follow the lake shore, until they came to a Frenchman's house. The boat departed, leaving Mr. Watson to his choice.

62 After the arrival of Colonel Hinman, Captain Baker took the command of a scout to discover the movements of the British troops at the isle *Aux Noix*. He cautiously landed at the bottom of a bay four miles above that island, in the silent watch of the night, there secured his boat, and in the morning went with his men on a point of land, whence he could see the said island and the lake for some distance. Baker being a curious marksman, always kept his musket in the best order possible, sat down and sharpened his flint; a party of Indians having discovered his boat, took and set off with it towards St. John's. Baker saw them approaching the point of land where he was. He stationed his men behind trees, and when the Indians came near he hailed them, and desired them to give up his boat in a friendly manner, as there was no war between the Indians and Americans. Baker had ordered his men to be concealed and ready, but not to fire on the Indians unless he did; the Indians showed no signs of giving up the boat, whereupon Baker ordered them to return his boat, or he would fire upon them. An Indian in the boat was preparing to fire on Baker, who attempted to fire before hand with him, but his musket missed fire, owing to the sharpness of his flint, which hitched on the steel; he recovered his piece, and again levelled it at the Indian, at which Instant the Indian fired at him, one buck shot entered his brains, and Baker fell dead on the spot. His men fired on the Indians, and wounded some, but the boat was 63 soon out of gun shot. Afterwards the Indians returned and cut off Baker's head, then carried it in triumph to St. John's, where the British officers bought and buried it; the body was
likewise

likewise interred.   Captain Baker was the first man killed in the
northern department, and being a gentleman universally respected,
his death made more noise in the country than the loss of a thous-
and men towards the end of the American war.

The district of the New Hampshire grants furnished a regiment
for the northern army, under the command of General Philip
Schuyler, who left the army at the Isle *Aux Noix*, and the command devolved on Brigadier-General Richard Montgomery.   Soon
after the blockade of Fort St. John's and the capture of Fort
Chamblee by Colonel John Brown, (where the Americans found a
considerable quantity of gun-powder, which, with the cannon, mor-
tars, shells, and shot, taken at Ticondaroga and Crownpoint, they
used in the forty-eight days siege at St. John's,) Colonels Allen,
Brown, and Warner were sent by General Montgomery into Canada, with small detachments, to learn the disposition of the Canadians, and the strength of Montreal.   They met on the east side
of the river St. Lawrence, opposite Montreal, where, in council,
it was agreed to attack that town.   Boats being scarce, it was
agreed, that Colonel Allen, with his party, should cross at Longuale, below Montreal, and Colonels Brown and Warner were to
cross from Laprairie, above the town.   The night for cross-
64 ing was agreed on, and the manner of proceeding.   The two
parties being nine miles distant from one another, they agreed,
upon principles of honour, that if any event should hinder either
party crossing at the hour appointed, early notice should be given
to the other.   The night proved windy, and Brown and Warner
judged it dangerous to attempt crossing the river, and went quietly
to rest, without sending any express to Colonel Allen, who apprehended no danger from the wind, therefore crossed the river with
his men, at different times, in the few small boats he had in his
possession.   The conduct of Brown and Warner is hard to be
accounted for, on any principles honourable to themselves.   We
are informed by sacred writ that *the disciples of Jesus Christ disputed among themselves who should be the greatest.*[1]   In the morn-

---

[1] [There could have been no proper foundation for the suspicion of
the author here intimated.   Under such an engagement with Allen,
both Brown and Warner would have every motive to perform their part
of it, as they would share equally with him in the honor of the capture
of the city.   Probably the author is mistaken in supposing that Col.
Warner was any way concerned in the attempt.   Col. Ethan Allen in
his narrative of his captivity represents the agreement to attack Montreal as having been made wholly with Brown, and makes no mention of
Warner, nor does he say any thing of an agreement to give notice of the
                                                              ing

ing the British troops and militia of Montreal marched against
Colonel Allen, who had chose the best ground for defence, and
put his men in order for battle, expecting Brown and Warner
every moment to his relief. The action commenced and continued
obstinate for a considerable time, but Brown and Warner not ap-
pearing, and Captain Young, with a number of Canadians, de-
serting, Colonel Allen and his small party, were overpowered, and
obliged to surrender themselves prisoners of war, on verbal stipulations with an officer, a natural son of Sir William Johnson, to
whom Colonel Allen gave his sword. As soon as he had parted
with his sword and musket, two Indians, painted in a fright-
65 ful manner, came up, and attempted to tomahawk Colonel
Allen, who, being a stout and strong man, seized the young *col-
oured officer*, a small man, and kept him as a target between himself and the Indians, which served for a defence till some British
officers ran to his relief.

In this action numbers were killed and wounded on both sides.
After the prisoners were conducted into Montreal, General Prescot gave orders to a serjeant and file of men to put to death some
Canadians who had been taken in arms with Colonel Allen; they
forthwith went, with their bayonets fixed, to execute the Canadians, according to the cowardly order of their General. Colonel Allen, understanding their business, stepped between them
and the Canadians, opened his bosom, and told the guard to thrust
their bayonets into his breast, if they must shed human blood,
and thereby save those poor Canadians, who deserved no cen-
sure, *as what they had done was in obedience to his orders.* The
guard were deterred, and returned to their General, whose or-

---

failure of either party to cross "at the hour appointed," which, indeed,
would seem to have been quite impracticable at nine miles distance.
The failure of Brown to unite in the attack may have been occasioned
by the great severity of the storm, at Lapraire, or by some other unexpected occurrence, which so frequently in military military operations
interposes to prevent the success of apparently well planned expeditions,
where success, as in this case, depends upon the united assault from distant points of different bodies of men. Both Brown and Warner had
deceased long before the publication of this work. Col. Brown was
killed in the Mohawk Valley, in 1780, in a battle with Canadians and
Indians, and Col. Warner died in 1784. Both left highly honorable military records. For an account of Col. Brown, see *Allen's Am. Biograph-
ical Dictionary.* Col. Warner's reputation is too well known to need
further notice here.]

ders

ders were re-considered.* The regiment of Vermonteers, com-
66 manded by Colonel Warner, was stationed at La Prairie and
Longuale, during the siege of St. John's; their duty was
67 severe, as they were daily exposed to the attacks from the
British at Montreal, therefore two companies of New York

* Colonel Allen, instead of receiving liberal usage, was *confined in irons* by a British General's order, and sent to Quebec. After much ill treatment there, he was sent on board a man of war, commanded by Captain Littlejohn, who acted with lenity and honour, for he ordered Colonel Allen to be liberated from his irons, except when military officers on shore came on board. While in this situation, a dispute arose between Captain Littlejohn and an officer; a challenge ensued; Captain Littlejohn called on Colonel Allen to serve as his friend; the Colonel answered, *if it was consistent in his situation, he would do himself the honor,* to which the Captain replied, *that he could change his dress, and go on shore in disguise, and no questions would be asked.* This measure was taken, but by the interposition of friends, the dispute was settled, and Captain Littlejohn and Colonel Allen returned to the ship. During Colonel Allen's captivity, he was put on board a man of war commanded by a Captain Smith, and confined in irons in the most dreary part of the ship; when the ship was got to sea, Captain Smith ordered Colonel Allen's irons off, requesting him to dine at his table that day, and in future, while on ship-board. Colonel Allen came on deck from his dark abode, thanked Captain Smith for his generous conduct, and said, *that he did not know it would ever be in his power to return the compliment;* Captain Smith replied, *that gentlemen did not know when they might render essential services to one another.* On board were a great number of prisoners, who laid a plan to kill Captain Smith, and run off with the ship. This plan being nearly ripe for execution, Colonel Allen was let into the secret, who told them if they murdered the Captain, they must also murder him, at which the conspirators were extremely alarmed, but Colonel Allen quieted them by saying, *drop your plan, and I will be as faithful to you as I have been to Captain Smith;* here the business ended, and Captain Smith never knew his danger, or the service of his grateful friend. While Colonel Allen was a prisoner to the British, he was imprisoned at Halifax, at Pendennis Castle, in Cornwall, where he applied for a writ of *Habeas Corpus* to be removed to London for trial; to prevent it he was put on board a man of war, and removed to Ireland, where he remained some time in the Cove of Cork, and received great civilities and many presents in money and stores, till he refused taking any more, but the Captain of the ship had the meanness to take the most of them from him. Afterwards he was sent to the prison at New York, and confined in irons, and experienced severe trials and hardships during near three years captivity, and then was exchanged for Colonel Campbell.

troops

troops were sent to reinforce them. General Carleton was busy in sending out boats to alarm Colonel Warner's party, and shot were daily exchanged between them near Longuale.

On this ground, Warner made several applications to General Montgomery, for some field-pieces, without success; at length the officers united in a petition for two field-pieces; fortunately they were sent, and arrived late in the evening. The next day General Carleton appeared with a large number of boats and men, with a view to land, march, and raise the siege of St. John's. Captain Potter was sent, with his company, nearly opposite to Grant's Island, where he arrived in time to prevent a party of Indians landing, and, after a smart skirmish, remained master of the ground, they retiring, with the loss of three prisoners, and four killed on the spot.

In the meantime a party of the enemy, in boats, took the advantage of the wind and current, and fell down against the town, where they expected to make good their landing, but were disappointed by a company of reserve, who marched down to the edge of the river before their two field-pieces, where they opened to the right and left, and discharged grapeshot upon the boats, which caused the enemy to believe a reinforcement had arrived, and, thus deceived, they gave Colonel Warner a victory over more than double his number of troops. Next morning Captain Heman Allen was sent with dispatches, and the three prisoners, to General Montgomery, who, after receiving them, sent a flag to Major Preston, Commandant at St. John's, and an account of the defeat of General Carleton, with the name of one of the prisoners, a man of consequence. Major Preston returned the flag, requesting a cessation of hostilities, and that the prisoner named might be permitted, on his parole of honour, to come into the garrison, and stay two hours.

The requests were granted, and the articles of capitulation were settled without further bloodshed. The garrison, consisting of about six hundred men, who surrendered prisoners of war, were almost destitute of provisions.

General Montgomery having ordered a gun-boat, with one nine-pounder in its bow, and other boats with field-pieces to Sorel, marched his army against Montreal. General Carleton, therefore, evacuated that city; his troops and a quantity of gunpowder were placed in eleven small vessels, which sailed for Quebec, but before they reached Sorel, a battery was erected there

there by the Americans, and two cannons mounted; besides, the gun-boat from St. John's had arrived in the River St. Lawrence. Doctor Jonas Fay wrote a spirited letter, demanding an immediate surrender of the fleet, without any demolition of the stores, stating also, that he was strongly posted at Sorel; Colonel James Easton signed the letter, and the writer was the bearer, with the flag. General Carleton seeing the battery and gun-boat, and a large number of troops on the shores, stopped the fleet, and returned the flag, with an answer to Colonel Easton. By this time Colonel Brown had arrived, who, with Dr. Fay, went on board the fleet with a second flag, and a truce was concluded on till next morning. In the night, however, General Carleton put himself into a small birch canoe, and, being covered with straw, was carried past Sorel by a Canadian, who, for this service, was allowed a pension of £82 sterling per annum during life. After this escape, the General proceeded on to Quebec with less danger, where he arrived safe. Next day the fleet was surrendered, and sent back to Montreal, where General Prescot, with the British troops, grounded their arms, and became prisoners of war. The Americans who were in the battery at Sorel, and on board the gun-boat, did not exceed 80 men, while those of the enemy, who
70 amounted to five times that number, with General Carleton at their head, were intimidated, and returned to Montreal, without attempting either to dislodge the Americans, or to pass them, which could have been done without much danger, either from the battery or gun-boat, as the wind and current favoured their descent. Thus, after the surrender of Fort St. John's, General Montgomery made himself master of the fleet and Montreal, without firing a single shot.

Colonel Warner's regiment having served out the time for which they enlisted, were dismissed, and went home. General Montgomery, with his army, proceeded to Quebec, with intentions to take that garrison, where he reinforced a detachment from Massachusetts under Colonel Benedict Arnold, who set out from Cambridge, went to the province of Main, ascended the river Kenebeck, descended the *Schedeure*, and formed the blockade of Quebec, after many hardships from hunger and cold in traversing a wilderness of some hundred miles, in an inclement season; here he was joined by General Montgomery, who took the command. The united forces erected batteries, and about the eighth of December commenced a tremendous cannonade and bombardment against that fortress, until their powder, shot, and shells were nearly exhausted, when, in a council of war, it was resolved to attempt to take the garrison by storm, though contrary to the opinion

71 ion of the General. The assault was agreed on, and accordingly commenced before day-light in the morning of the first of January, 1776, and proved unsuccessful ; the General was killed, and the assailants repulsed with the loss of a considerable number of men. The command then devolved on Colonel Benedict Arnold, who had received a ball, under the walls of Quebec, in his leg ; the siege was continued with perseverance, in this inhospitable and frozen clime, during the winter and spring, until the 6th of May following, under many and complicated discouragements. In this dilemma, the district of the New-Hampshire Grants raised a second regiment under Colonel Warner, which marched to Quebec soon after the death of General Montgomery ; the reinforcements which arrived from Montreal, and Colonel Warner's regiment, gave essential relief to the besieging army of a strong citadel.

On the 6th of May the siege was raised, in consequence of the arrival of a British fleet with considerable reinforcements, and the assailants were compelled to retreat from that place ; the small-pox and a camp distemper raged in the army, which was in a bad state of health and spirits. General Thompson, and a detachment under his command, were defeated in an action, near *Trois Rivieres*, with considerable loss of killed, wounded, and prisoners. General Sullivan, on the whole, however, made a retreat that would have done honour to an officer of greater experi-
72 ence, being almost continuously harassed by the enemy ; after many difficulties the army arrived at Crown Point in a deplorable state.

This disastrous retreat exposed the frontiers of the New Hampshire Grants to an invasive war ; most of the inhabitants on Onion river and the shores of Champlain, north of Crown Point, instantly removed, and the militia was organized by the Convention of the New Hampshire Grants. The best possible measures for defence were taken, carefully guarding against all connections with the provincial Congress and Committees of New York. Several conferences were held among the leaders of the people, concerning the establishment of civil government ; some were for returning and joining with New Hampshire, supposing that would secure the titles of their lands, notwithstanding the subsequent and illegal grants of the Governor of New York ; others were disposed to form a new State, including all the district of the New Hampshire Grants west of Connecticut river, while some were for joining with New York during the war ; this idea too much affected the property of the settlers. For the time being as liberty
was

was the reigning passion, they cordially united in self-defence and in the support of Congress, and accordingly, to evince their attachment to the general cause, met at Dorset in convention, Jan. 1776, and drew up a petition to Congress, and which was the first application of the people to that body, stiled " the humble Petition,

73 Address, and Remonstrance of that part of America, being situate south of Canada line, west of Connecticut river, commonly called and known by the name of the New Hampshire Grants," in which they avowed their readiness at all times to furnish their quota in support of the war, not only by raising troops, but but by bearing an equal proportion with the other colonies, in defence of the rights and liberties of the American people. The Committee of Congress, to whom this application was referred, reported as their opinion, " that it be recommended " to the Petitioners for the present, to submit to the Government " of New York, and to assist their countrymen in the contest " with Great Britain ; but that such submission ought not to prej- " udice their right to any lands in controversy, or be construed " to affirm or admit the jurisdiction of New York over the coun- " try, when the present troubles should be ended ;* " however to avoid a decision, it was thought advisable to withdraw the petition.

Colonel Allen being in captivity, Baker dead, Warner, Cockran, and others engaged in the army, greatly weakened the Council of the enterprizers of the New Hampshire Grants, and some months passed without any decisive measures being taken. The people had been governed by committees and conventions as before the war, with this difference, the dispute with the Governor and Coun-

74 cil of New York seemed to be lost in the common cause of the struggling colonies of America ; for those who had been outlawed and indicted for high treason, riots and sedition against the authority of New York, passed freely, and without any kind of molestation through the colony of New York.

In the beginning of the year 1776, four of the leading men conferred on measures to be recommended to the people for the establishment of a civil Government, which appeared necessary effectually to carry on the war, raise men and money, and to secure the titles of the lands against the latent intentions of the Governor of New York : Those men differed in opinion about a plan, though all were convinced that their and the country's interest required a connection with New Hampshire, or an establishment of a new government ; no one of them dreamed of ever associating with

* *Williams's History of Vermont.*

New

New York, whose late persecuting conduct and system of government, rendered that colony the most detestable of any on earth.

The arguments advanced in favour of a union with New Hampshire were, that as the jurisdiction of the New Hampshire Grants had been transferred from that colony through the misrepresentations of the Governor and Council of New York (contrary to the interest and wish of the settlers, who held their lands under Royal deeds from New Hampshire,) a petition from the settlers to the Governor and Council of New Hampshire, praying them 75 to extend their jurisdiction over them as formerly, notwithstanding the order of the King and Privy Council, would be granted, and the settlers would be gratified, and unite cordially in carrying on the war. That such a union would be highly satisfactory to the people of New England, whose children were settled on the grants, and many owned lands there under New Hampshire titles; and that this measure would secure all those who held lands under the grants of New Hampshire, and avoid a dispute with Congress respecting a new State, which the envy and intrigues of New York and the calamities of war might produce.

The arguments in favour of a new Government were, they did not like any connection with a colony, which, by act of a royal Governor, had too easily consented to part with territory, contrary to the interest and wishes of the people, and who might hereafter expose themselves to the evil intentions of the colony of New York. That by such a connection they should lose all the glory and credit they had gained in their exertions against the Governor and Council of New York. That a new Government would perpetuate the name of the Green Mountain Boys, and the honour of their leaders. That a new Government would infallibly establish the title of their lands under the New Hampshire Grants; and that the unappropriated lands might be disposed 76 of to defray the expences of Government and the war. That as a separate Government, in the course of events, they might find ways and means to retaliate on the monopolists of New York, who had given them so much trouble in re-granting and claiming the lands they held and occupied under the grants of New Hampshire. That the active and offensive part taken at an early period of the war, in taking Ticonderoga, Crown Point and St. John's, would make them consequential in the eyes of Congress, as friends to the American revolution. That nothwithstanding the influence of New York might for a time prevent the new Government from a representation in Congress, yet it might not eventually hurt the interest of the people. That the district of the New Hampshire
Grants

Grants, on revolutionary principles, was the *oldest* in America.
That the people had governed themselves by Committees of Safety
and Conventions, against the oppressions and tyranny of New
York, eight years before the colonies of America took similar
measures against Great Britain; of course the people ought to
persevere and brave every danger that might be in the womb of
futurity. The result of those deliberations was to establish a new
Government; accordingly great care was taken to prepare the
minds of the people for such an event, and to effect the important
object; circular letters were sent to convene a Convention at Dorset, on the 24th of July, 1776; fortunately for these measures,
Congress, on the 4th of the same month, made and published
77 their declaration of independence of the colonies on Great
Britain, declaring them to be free and independent states, which
appeared, and was announced by the public papers to the people
of the grants, a few days before the meeting of the Convention.

In this Convention thirty-five towns were represented, and consisted of fifty-one members, who unanimously were opposed to
any connection with the Committees or provincial Congress of
New York, and drew up an association for the support of the
rights and liberties of the people, considering any who formed an
association with the Congress of New York, as enemies to the
common cause, which association was signed by all the members
of the Convention, and sent to the several towns for signatures.
The Convention appointed Heman Allen, Jonas Fay, and William
Marsh to be a Committee to visit each town in the counties of
Cumberland and Gloucester, to invite the people to unite in forming a new State, and for that purpose to send members to the
Convention to be convened at Dorset, in September. The Convention accordingly met, and were joined by several members from
the aforementoined counties, when it was unanimously resolved,
that the district of the New Hampshire Grants, ought, of right, to
be a free and independent state; and that they had the same right
so to be, as Congress had to declare the colonies independent of
the King and Parliament of Great Britain. They appointed
78 William Marsh and Ira Allen their Committee to visit the
counties of Cumberland and Gloucester, to point out to the people
the advantages which would result from the district of the grants
becoming a free state. They adjourned to meet at Westminster, in
November,[1] who met at the time and place aforesaid, and it appeared that great part of the people were ripe for a *new state*,
but an obstacle appeared in the way, occasioned by the influence

---

[1] [The adjournment was to the 30th of October.]

of

of the Congress of New York. The Convention continued Marsh
and Allen their Committee, and adjourned to January, 1777.

The Representatives from the several towns on both sides of the
mountain, met in January at Westminster, and deliberately debated, for and against the formation of a new state. After mature deliberation, the members were of opinion, that the interest
and safety of the people required the district of the New Hampshire Grants to be a free state. That the power of Government
was vested in the people by the supreme arbiter of rights. That
the people had not delegated their natural right of chusing what
form of government they should be governed by, to any King,
State, or Potentate on earth ; and that they therefore had the
right and power, and would henceforth use and exercise the right
and power of government vested in them by the beneficent Creator.
On the 15th of January, 1777, the Convention published the following declaration, "This Convention, whose members are duly
79 " chosen by the free voice of their Constituents, in the several
" towns on the New Hampshire Grants, in public meeting as-
" sembled, in our names, and in behalf of our Constituents, do
" hereby proclaim, and publicly declare, that the district of ter-
" ritory, comprehending, and usually known by the name and
" description of the New Hampshire Grants, of right ought to be,
" and is hereby declared, forever hereafter to be considered as a
" free and independent jurisdiction or state ; to be forever here-
" after called, known, and distinguished by the name of *New*
" *Connecticut*, and that the inhabitants that are at present, or
" that may hereafter become resident within said territory, shall
" be entitled to the same privileges, immunities, and enfranchise-
" ments, which are, or that may at any time hereafter be allowed
" to the inhabitants of any of the free and independent states of
" America ; and that such privilege and immunities shall be reg-
" ulated in a bill of rights, and by a form of government to be
" established at the next sessions of this Convention." A Committee to inform Congress of this declaration, was appointed, and
repaired to Philadelphia, consisting of four persons, who presented
the following *declaration* and *petition* to that body, stiled

80 " *The Declaration and Petition of the Inhabitants of the New
Hampshire Grants, to Congress, announcing the District to
be a Free and Independent State.*

" To the Honourable the CONTINENTAL CONGRESS.

" THE Declaration and Petition of that part of North America,
situate south of Canada line, west of Connecticut river, north of
the

the Massachusetts Bay, and east of a twenty-mile line from Hudson's river, containing about one hundred and forty-four townships, of the contents of six miles square, each granted your petitioners by the authority of New Hampshire, besides several grants made by the authority of New York, and a quantity of vacant land, humbly sheweth,

" That your petitioners, by virtue of several grants made them by the authority aforesaid, have many years since, with their families, become actual settlers and inhabitants of the said described premises, by which it is now become a respectable frontier to three neighboring states, and is of great importance to our common barrier Ticonderoga, as it has furnished the army there with much provisions, and can muster more than five thousand hardy soldiers, capable of bearing arms in defence of American liberty.

" That shortly after your petitioners began their settlements, a 81 party of land-jobbers in the city and state of New York began to claim the lands, and took measures to have them declared to be within that jurisdiction.

" That on the 4th day of July, 1764, the King of Great Britain did pass an order in Council, extending the jurisdiction of the New York Government to Connecticut river, in consequence of a representation made by the late Lieutenant-Governor Colden ; that for the convenience of trade, and administration of justice, the inhabitants were desirous of being annexed to that State.

" That on this alteration of jurisdiction, the said Lieutenant-Governor Colden did grant several tracts of land in the above described limits, to certain persons living in the State of New York, which were at that time in the actual possession of your petitioners ; and under colour of the lawful authority of said State, did proceed against your petitioners, as lawless intruders upon the Crown lands in their province. This produced an application to the King of Great Britain, from your petitioners, setting forth their claims under the Government of New Hampshire, and the disturbance and interruption they had suffered from said post claimants, under New York. And on the 24th day of July, 1767, an order was passed at St. James's, prohibiting the Governors of New York, for the time being, from granting any part of the described premises, on pain of incurring his highest displeasure. 83 Nevertheless the same Lieutenant-Governor Colden, Governors Dunmore and Tryon, have each and every of them, in their respective

respective turns of administration, presumed to violate the said royal order, by making several grants of the prohibited premises, and countenancing an actual invasion of your petitioners, by force of arms, to drive them off from their possessions.

"Those violent proceedings, (with the solemn declaration of the supreme court of New York, that the charters, conveyances, &c. of your petitioners' lands, were utterly null and void, on which they were founded,) reduced your petitioners to the disagreeable necessity of taking up arms, as the only means left for the security of their possessions. The consequence of this step was the passing twelve acts of outlawry, by the legislature of New York, on the ninth day of March, 1774, which were not intended for the State in general, but only for part of the counties of Albany and Charlotte, viz. such parts thereof as are covered by the New Hampshire charters.

"Your petitioners having had no representative in that assembly, when these acts were passed, they first came to the knowledge of them by public newspapers, in which they were inserted. By these, they were informed, that if three or more of them assembled together to oppose what said assembly called legal authority, that such as should be found assembled, to the number of three or more, should be adjudged felons: And that in case they, or any of them, should not surrender himself or themselves, to certain officers appointed for the purpose of securing them, after a warning of seventy days, that then it should be lawful for the respective Judges of the Supreme Court of the province of New York, to award execution of *Death*, the same as though he or they had been attainted before a proper Court of Judicatory. These laws were evidently calculated to intimidate your petitioners into a tame surrender of their rights, and such a state of vassalage, as would entail misery on their latest posterity.

83

"It appears to your petitioners then, an infringement on their rights is still meditated by the state of New York; as we find in their general Convention at Harlem, the second day of August last, it was unanimously voted ' That all quit-rents formerly due and owing to the crown of Great Britain within this State, are now due and owing to this Convention, or such future government as may hereafter be established in this state.'

"By a submission to the claims of New York, your petitioners would be subjected to the payment of two shillings and sixpence sterling on every hundred acres annually, which, compared with the

the quit-rents of Levingston's, Phillips's, and Ranslear's manors, and many other enormous tracts in the best situations in the State, 84 would lay the most disproportionate share of the public expence on your petitioners, in all respects the least able to bear it.

" The Convention of New York have now nearly completed a code of laws, for the future government of that State; which, should they be attempted to be put in execution, will subject your petitioners to the fatal necessity of opposing them by every means in their power.

" When the declaration of the honourable the Continental Congress of the fourth of July last past, reached your petitioners, they communicated it throughout the whole of their district; and being properly apprized of the proposed meeting, delegates from the several counties and towns in the district, described in the preamble to this petition, did meet at Westminster, in said district, and after several adjournments, for the purpose of forming themselves into a distinct and separate State, did make and publish a declaration, 'that they would at all times hereafter consider themselves as a free and independent State, capable of regulating their own internal police, in all and every respect whatsoever; and that the people in the said described district, have the sole exclusive right of governing themselves in such a manner and form, as they in their wisdom should choose; not repugnant to any resolves of the honourable the Continental Congress:' And for the mutual support of each other in the maintenance of the freedom and independence of the said district or separate State, the said 85 delegates did jointly and severally pledge themselves to each other, by all the ties that are held sacred among men, and resolve and declare, that they were at all times ready, in conjunction with their brethren of the United States, to contribute their full porportion towards maintaining the present just war against the fleets and armies of Great Britain.

" To convey this declaration and resolution to your honourable body, the grand Representative of the United States, were we (your more immediate petitioners) delegated by the united and unanimous voice of the Representatives of the whole body of the settlers on the described premises, in whose name and behalf, We humbly pray, that the said declaration may be received, and the district described therein may be ranked by your Honours among the free and independent American States, and Delegates therefrom

from admitted to seats in the grand Continental Congress, and your Petitioners, as in duty bound, shall ever pray.

" *New Hampshire Grants, Westminster,*
15*th* Jan. 1777.

" Signed by order and in behalf of said inhabitants,

JONAS FAY.
THOMAS CHITTENDEN.
HEMAN ALLEN.
REUBEN JONES."

86   Fay, Chittenden, Allen, and Jones, returned from Congress, without the decision of that body upon their petition in behalf of the inhabitants, and brought with them Dr. Young's letter, printed and published at Philadelphia, addressed to the inhabitants of *Vermont*,* and among others were these paragraphs : " I have taken the minds of several leading members in the hon- " ourable the Continental Congress, and can assure you, that you " have nothing to do but to send attested copies of the recommen- " dation to take up Government to every township in your dis- " trict, and invite all your freeholders and inhabitants to meet in " their respective townships, and choose members for a General " Convention, to meet at an early day, to choose delegates for the " General Congress, a Committee of Safety, and to form a Con- " stitution for your State. Your friends here tell me, that some " are in doubt, whether delegates from your district would be ad- " mitted into Congress ; I tell you to organize fairly, and make 87 " the experiment, and I will ensure you success, at the risk " of my reputation as a man of honour or common sense ; in- " deed, they can by no means refuse you ; you have as good a " right to choose how you will be governed, and by whom, as they " had." Previous to this, and a few days after the declaration of the independence of the State of Vermont, the Convention of the State of New York was then sitting ; alarmed at the conse-

---

* *Vermont*, this name was given to the district of the New Hampshire Grants, as an emblematical one, from the French of *Verd-mont*, green mountains, intended to perpetuate the name of the Green Mountain Boys, by Dr. Thomas Young, of Philadelphia, who greatly interested himself in behalf of the settlers of Vermont, by several publications ; he was highly distinguised as a philosopher, philanthropist, and patriot, and for his erudition and brilliancy of imagination. His death was universally regretted by the friends of American Independence, as one of her warm supporters, and by the republic of letters as a brilliant ornament.

quences

quences which might result from such a measure, their President, by order of the Committee of Safety, wrote to Congress, January 20th, 1777, thus:

" I am directed by the Committee of Safety of New York, to inform Congress, that by the arts and influence of certain designing men, a part of this State hath been prevailed on to revolt, and disavow the authority of its legislature. The various evidences and informations we have received would lead us to believe that persons of great influence in some of our sister States have fostered and fomented these divisions. But as these informations tend to accuse some members of your honourable body, of being concerned in this scheme, decency obliges us to suspend our belief. The Convention are sorry to observe, that by conferring a commission upon Colonel Warner, with authority to name the officers of a regiment, to be raised independently of the legislature of this State, and within that part of it, which hath lately declared an independence upon it, Congress hath given but too much weight to the insinuations of those, who pretend that your honourable body are determined to support these insurgents; especially, as this Colonel Warner, hath been constantly and invariably opposed to the legislature of this State, and hath been, on that very account, proclaimed an outlaw by the late government thereof. It is absolutely necessary to recall the commissions given to Colonel Warner, and the officers under him, as nothing else will do justice to us, and convince those deluded people, that Congress have not been prevailed on to assist in dismembering a State, which of all others, has suffered the most in the common cause.* "

The Convention of New York, on the 1st of March following, again attempted to engage Congress to take up the matter, well knowing that the people of Vermont were daily becoming more formidable against the State of New York, and that they, by being permitted to exercise the functions of Government, would soon form a regular body, and be lost to that State. In this the Convention of New York represent, that they depend upon the justice of that honourable house, to adopt every wise and salutary expedient, to suppress the mischiefs which must ensue to that State and to the general confederacy, from the unjust and pernicious projects of such of the inhabitants of New York, as merely from selfish and interested motives, have fomented the dangerous insurrection: That Congress might be assured that the spirit of defection, notwithstanding all the arts and violence of

* Attested copy of a letter from the Honourable A. Ten Broek, President of the Convention of New York, dated January 20, 1777.

the

the seducers, was by no means general : That the county of Gloucester, and a very great part of Cumberland, and Charlotte counties, continued steadfast in their allegiance to the Government of
New York ; and that there was not the least probability that Colonel Warner could raise such a number of men, as would be an
object of public concern.* The publications and interest which
many persons seemed to take in behalf of the new State, was viewed with no less indignation than regret by the Convention of New
York, and on the 28th of May, the Council of Safety of that State,
directed their President again to write to Congress, complaining
to that body that they had reasons to conclude that numbers of
their body were concerned in an attempt to dismember the State,
" however unwilling we may be to entertain suspicions so disre-
" spectful to any members of Congress, yet the truth is, that no
" inconsiderable numbers of the people of this State do believe the
" report to be well founded ; " from this it appears that Vermont
had a considerable number of friends in Congress, notwithstand-
90 ing the unfavourable resolutions on their *declaration* and *petition* of the 15th of January, 1777, which was taken up by
Congress on the motion of a member from New York, who laid
before that body, on the 22d of June, the publication of Dr.
Young to the Inhabitants of Vermont; and on the 30th of the
same month passed the following resolves :

" *Resolved*, That Congress is composed of delegates chosen
by, and representing the communities respectively inhabiting the
territories of New Hampshire, Massachusetts Bay, Rhode Island
and Providence Plantations, Connecticut, New York, New Jersey,
Pennsylvania, Delaware, Maryland, Virginia, North Carolina,
South Carolina, and Georgia, as they respectively stood at the
time of its first institution ; that it was instituted for the purpose
of securing and defending the communities aforesaid, against the
usurpations, oppressions, and hostile invasions of Great Britain ;
and, therefore, it cannot be intended that Congress, by any of its
proceedings, would do, or recommend, or countenance, any thing
injurious to the rights and jurisdiction of the several communities,
which it represents.

" *Resolved*, That the independent Government attempted to be
established by the people, stiling themselves inhabitants of the
New Hampshire Grants, can derive no countenance or justifica-
91 tion from the act of Congress, declaring the united colonies
to be independent of the crown of Great Britain, nor from
any other act or resolution of Congress.

* Letter from A. Ten Broek, of March 1, 1777.

" *Resolved*,

" *Resolved*, That the petition of Jonas Fay, Thomas Chitten-den, Heman Allen, and Reuben Jones, in the name and behalf of the people, stiling themselves as aforesaid, praying that ' their declaration, that they would consider themselves as a free and independent State, may be received ; that the district in the said petition described, may be ranked among the free and independ-ent States ; and that delegates therefrom may be admitted to seats in Congress,' be dismissed.

" *Resolved*, That Congress, by raising and officering the regi-ment, commanded by Colonel Warner, never meant to give any encouragement to the claim of the people aforesaid, to be con-sidered as an independent State ; but that the reason which in-duced Congress to form that corps, was, that many officers of dif-ferent States, who had served in Canada, and alledged that they could soon raise a regiment, but were then unprovided for, might be reinstated in the service of the United States."

Having recited the paragraphs in the letter from Thomas Young, which have been quoted, they next resolve, " That the contents of the said paragraphs are derogatory to the honour of Congress, are a gross misrepresentation of the resolution of Congress therein referred to, and tend to deceive and mislead the people to whom they are addressed."

92

Soon after the return of the Commissioners from Congress, Ira Allen printed and published a pamphlet,[1] shewing the right the people had to form a Goverument, which, with Dr. Young's Let-ter, were spread through the State, and measures taken to con-vene a Convention, which met at Windsor in June 1777, to form a constitution, and appointed a committee to make a draft of a constitution, and passed a resolution, recommending it to each town to elect and send Representatives to a Convention, to meet at Windsor in July following.   William Marsh, James Mead, Ira Allen, and Captain Salisbury, were appointed a Committee to wait on the Commander of Ticondaroga Fort, and consult with him respecting the regulations and defence of the frontiers, then adjourned to the 4th[2] of July, 1777, to meet at the same place. While the Committee was at Ticondaroga, General Burgoyne, with his army, appeared on the lake, and resting at Crown Point, he sent a scout of about 300, mostly Indians, to land at the mouth

---

[1] [For a copy of this pamphlet, see *ante* p. 139.]

[2] [The adjournment to, and the meeting at Windsor were July 2, in-stead of the 4th.]

of

of Otter Creek, to annoy the frontiers of the State. General
Poor refused to allow any troops to the Committee for the defence
of the frontiers, but allowed Colonel Warner to go with the Committee, who soon raised men sufficient to repel the assailants. All
who were members of the Convention left the militia, and repaired to Windsor on July 4th,[1] 1777. A draft of a constitution was
93 laid before the Convention, and read. The business being
new, and of great consequence, required serious deliberation.
The Convention had it under consideration when the news of the
evacuation of Ticondaroga arrived, which alarmed them very much,
as thereby the frontiers of the State were exposed to the inroads of
an enemy. The family of the President of the Convention, as well
as those of many other members, were exposed to the foe. In
this awful crisis the Convention was for leaving Windsor, but a
severe thunder-storm came on, and gave them time to reflect,
while other members, less alarmed at the news, called the attention of the whole to finish the Constitution, which was then reading paragraph by paragraph for the last time. This was done,
and the Convention then appointed a Council of Safety to act
during the recess, and the Convention adjourned.

The Council of Safety proceeded to Manchester and on their
arrival found that to be Colonel Warner's head quarters, and that
he had only part of his regiment with him, which was raised in
Vermont. That Colonels Warner and Francis had brought up
the rear of the army in the retreat from Ticondaroga, and were
overtaken at Hubbardton by a party of the enemy, where a severe
skirmish took place, and just as the enemy began to give way,
Colonel Francis ordered a retreat of part of his regiment, to take
a more advantageous position; his orders were mistook, and the re-
94 treat was general; this encouraged the enemy, and Colonel
Francis, in endeavouring to stop the retreat and confusion of
his regiment, was killed; thus the enemy geined a battle, which a
few moments before had been given over as a defeat. The loss in
killed and wounded was considerable on both sides; in this dispute Colonel Warner's regiment suffered severely. Thus, in a
few days, the inhabitants, for near a hundred miles on the west
side of the Green Mountains, were left without protection by the
American army. General Redhasle, with his Hessian troops,
pushed on from Skeensborough to Castleton, where some of the
inhabitants took protection under him, while others fled with their
families, flocks and herds. The roads were, as well as the coun-

---

[1] [The adjournment to, and the meeting at Windsor were July 2, instead of the 4th.]

try,

try, a scene of confusion ; the inhabitants retiring southward, the army took a circuitous course more toward the west, and rendevouzed at Saratoga.

The Council of Safety adjourned to Sunderland, where Ira Allen, in behalf of the Council of Safety, wrote to Mr. Weare, President of New Hampshire, informing him of the evacuation of Ticondaroga, and the retreat and disastrous situation of the army, and the exposed situation of the inhabitants of Vermont, declaring, that unless speedily relieved, they would be obliged to evacuate great part of the State. A similar letter was sent to the Governor of Massachusett's, as it was discovered that the Generals of the army had not sent any expresses to either.

95 The Council of Safety then attended to the affairs of the Government, but their situation was very unpleasant, as the Convention had only declared the district to be a free State; but the Government was not organized, as the Constitution was not fully compleated, and near three quarters of the people on the west side of the Green Mountains were compelled to remove, and the rest were in great danger. It was they who principally supported the title of the New Hampshire Grants, against the unjust claims of New York, and their removal would expose the settlers on the east side of the Green Mountains to an invasive war, both from the Savages and the British ; besides, the late proceedings of Congress had been partial towards New York, and against Vermont ; the people of the new State had reason to expect no favour from the Committee of Safety of New York, as its members were in fact composed of the old sycophants of the late Government, which they prudently deserted. Gain and dominion were objects of the first consequence to some of the Committee of New York, and the citizens of the new State were conscious that they would take every sinister and possible step to divide the people, and would not be dissatisfied with any misfortune which befel them, even by the common enemy.

The Council of Safety had ro money or revenue at command, their powers and credit were not extensive, and all expresses were supported at their private expence ; yet, in this situation, it became necessary to raise men for the defence of the frontiers, with bounties and wages; ways and means were to be found out, and the day was spent in debating on the subject ; Nathan Clark, not convinced of the practicability of raising a regiment, moved in Council, that Mr. Ira Allen, the youngest member

member of Council, and who insisted on raising a regiment, while a majority of the Council were for only two companies, of sixty men each, might be requested to discover ways and means to raise and support a regiment, and to make his report at sun-rising on the morrow. The Council acquiesced, and Mr. Allen took the matter into consideration. Next morning, at sun-rising, the Council met, and he reported the ways and means to raise and support a regiment, viz. that the Council should appoint Commissioners of Sequestration, with authority to seize the goods and chattels of all persons who had or should join the common enemy; and that all property so seized should be sold at public vendue, and the proceeds paid to the Treasurer of the Council of Safety, for the purpose of paying the bounties and wages of a regiment forthwith to be raised for the defence of the State. The Council adopted the measure, and appointed officers for the regiment. Samuel Herrick, Esq; was appointed the Colonel, and the men inlisted, and the bounties paid in fifteen days, out of the confiscated property of the enemies of the new state. This was the first instance in America of seizing and selling the property of the enemies of American independence.

97

The Council adjourned to Bennington, and about the time this regiment was raising, a party of militia from Massachusett's arrived in the new State. General Schuyler, a citizen of the State of New York, and Commander in Chief of the northern army, no sooner heard of it, than he sent orders to the militia of Massachusett's, and to Colonel Herrick's regiment, to repair forthwith to Saratoga; the militia from Massachusett's were obliged to obey, according to the regulations of the Continental Congress; but the Council of Safety superceded General Schuyler's orders, and gave special directions to Colonel Herrick to remain within the State of Vermont. This occasioned some irascible letters between General Schuyler and the Council of Safety, which were terminated by a peremptory order of Council to Colonel Herrick not to put himself under the command of General Schuyler.

The General Court of New Hampshire, in consequence of the evacuation of Ticondaroga, appointed Colonel John Starks a Brigadier General, and instructed him to go with his troops and join the northern army for the defence of the frontiers. General Starks informed the General Court, that he was ready and willing to act in concert with the Green Mountain Boys in defence of the frontiers, but could not think it his duty to put himself under the command of General Schuyler, or any other continental officer. The President of New Hampshire in vain argued against the

98

the reasons of General Starks, who offered to give up his commission ; but finally, the President and Council left it optional with General Starks, whether to be commanded or not by any continental officer.	General Starks received orders to " repair to " Charlestown, on Connecticut River ; there to consult with a " Committee of the New Hampshire Grants, respecting his future " operations, and the supply of his men with provisions ; to take " the command of the militia, and march into the Grants, to act " in conjunction with the troops of that new State, or any other " of the States, or of the United States*."	On his arrival at Charlestown, he wrote to Ira Allen, Esq. for advice and directions from the Council of Safety, respecting his future rout and stores. Mr. Allen, by order of the Council, advised General Starks to take the direct road to Manchester, and to hasten his march as much as possible, and join with Colonel Warner's regiment.	Mr. Allen also informed General Starks, that Vermont had raised a regiment of Rangers, under Colonel Herrick, who would be ready to assist.	General Starks, on his arrival at Manchester, met orders from General Schuyler, directing him to march and join the army at Saratoga.	This order was rejected, and the express returned.	General Schuyler then sent a positive order, and General Starks returned an absolute refusal, alledging his orders from the President and Council of New Hampshire to join or not under the command of a continental officer†.	In the mean time,

99

* Belknap's History of New Hampshire.

† The author of this History, in 1779, being at Exeter, was informed by Mr. Thompson, Member and Secretary of the Council of New Hampshire, that Generals Poor and Starks were Captains at the reduction of Canada in 1761, and that in 1775, they were on the same day appointed Colonels; that in 1776, Colonel Poor was appointed Brigadier General, at which Colonel Starks was offended, and declined service, observing *that in* 1777, *a powerful army would come from the north, which he, with the Green Mountain Boys, would cut off wing by wing.* After General Starks had refused to obey the orders of General Schuyler, and justified his conduct by his instructions, General Schuyler complained to Congress of the Orders of the Council of New Hampshire. A severe reprimand, of course, was sent to the Council. A Committee of the Council, (Mr. Thompson being one) was appointed to return an answer to Congress. They could not find at that time sufficient reasons to justify their instructions to General Starks, and therefore delayed their answer for a few days, when the news of General Starks's victories over two detachments of the royal army at Bennington arrived, the Committee were able to send a satisfactory answer to Congress for giving such optional instructions to General Starks, who had, with the Green Mountain Boys, laid a foundation to surround

Mr.

100 Mr. Chittenden, the President of the Council of Safety of Vermont, corresponded with General Starks, and had received information that a detachment from General Burgoyne's army was on its march to Bennington; they rested at Walloomscoick, near the line of that town, and in three days threw up a breastwork with logs and earth, on an advantageous height, nearly five feet high. During those three days, every possible preparation was made by the Council of Safety and General Starks for a battle with the detachment under Colonel *Bawn*. The 17th day of August, 1777, was fixed on for the attack by General Starks, and Colonel Warner was to remain at Manchester as long as he conveniently could, and be timely to the support of General Starks; it was concluded that too great movements would alarm Colonel Bawm, and cause him to retrogade. On the evening of the 15th, General Starks had under his command nearly the same number of undisciplined troops from New Hampshire and Vermont, including a few from Berkshire county, as Colonel Bawm had of disciplined troops in his breast-works, with four brass field-pieces. General Starks received information from the Council of Safety, that in another day, Colonel Bawm would be joined by a detachment on its way to reinforce him under the command of Colonel Skene, and thereby his numbers would be double, and his own could not be increased in the same proportion; he, therefore, resolved to make the assault on the 16th, and an express was sent to Colonel Warner with the determination; accordingly

101 preparations were made, and the assault commenced on all sides of the breast-work at the same time. The firing was promiscuous by the marksmen at every man who appeared above the breast-work; this method proved efficacious, and terrified the enemy to such a degree, that the assailants soon became masters of the breast-work, and took a number of prisoners, their field-pieces, and baggage; those who escaped from the breast-work were pursued, 'till they met the detachment under Colonel Skene; Colonel Herrick then retreated before Colonel Skene. At this critical moment Colonel Warner arrived with his regiment,[1] and enabled General Starks to go forward with the four field-pieces just taken from Colonel Bawm, against Colonel Skene, who was

and capture General Burgoyne and his whole army, which soon followed, and Congress were content, and honoured General Starks with the commission of a Brigadier General in the army of the United States.

---

[1] [Col. Warner himself was with Stark before and during the first battle. His regiment arrived late as stated above. See Gen. Stark's letter to Gen. Gates, *ante* p. 206; also p. 209.]

soon

soon defeated, made a precipitate retreat, and being favoured by the
night, made their escape, and rejoined the royal army. Colonel
Skene had his horse killed under him, and immediately mounted
on another, and being hard pressed, retreated with the remains of
two detachments from Burgoyne's army, (either of which were
equal in number to General Starks's whole force.)   In both bat-
tles the British lost in killed about 300 men, wounded and made
prisoners about 750.   General Starks had only about 50 killed,
some wounded, who afterwards died of their wounds. Heman
Allen, Esq. a member of the Council of Safety of Vermont, went
to the field of battle ; the weather being hot, and his fatigue great,
102 he caught a violent cold, and died of a decline on the 18th
     of May following.

Before this battle, heaviness and a dark cloud hung over the
northern States.   General Burgoyne's army was large, and had
been victorious in every place, and his proclamations breathed
forth many threatenings, and, in addition, the highest *confidence*
was not placed by the people in General Scuyler.   In verity, it
was the time that tried the fortitude and spirits of all men, among
whom none but the true-born sons of liberty and perseverance
could brave the danger of taking arms in so critical a time.   The
Green Mountain Boys were deeply interested in the fate of the
day ; for the very existence of the infant State of Vermont, their
families, and property, were all pending on the event.   Colonel
Bawm was killed in the first action, and orders from General Burgoyne were found in his pockets, which shew how the Government of Great Britain, and their officers, were deceived with respect to America.   By those orders Colonel Bawm was to have
proceeded to Bennington and burn the continental stores, thence
take the road to Newbury, on Connecticut River, and down the
river to Brattleboro', thence to return and rejoin the main army.
To have fullfilled his orders he must, with his army, field-pieces,
ammunition, and baggage, have travelled thirty miles a day, and
have twice crossed the Green Mountains, in roads scarcely passa-
103 ble with a single horse, and find horses to mount his *cavalry*
     and beeves for his army, and, besides, traversing this part
of New England, was truly taking the bull by the horns.   The
Assembly of Connecticut, at this time, was sitting at Hartford,
and General Sir Henry Clinton was moving his army up the
North River to join General Burgoyne.   The Legislature of Connecticut was informed, that the continental stores and meeting-
house at Bennington were burnt by the British, and the Green
Mountain Boys had been defeated with great loss ; in this conster-
nation the Assembly knew not how to direct their militia, and ad-
                                                              journed

journed 'till the afternoon. When they had met in the afternoon, they seemed not determined in any matter, until an express arrived that announced the two victories gained by General Starks, with an account of the killed and the prisoners, who were safely lodged in the meeting-house, which they were informed a few hours before, was burnt. The Assembly were no longer at a loss how to direct its militia. Colonel Willet soon after obtained a victory on the Mohock River over another detachment, under the command of Colonel St. Ledger, from Canada, and which intended to have formed a junction with General Burgoyne on the Hudson's River. These victories presaged the capture of General Burgoyne and his army. Soon after the battle of Bennington, a plan was laid to cut off General Burgoyne's communication with Canada, by means of Fort Ticondaroga. To effect this, General Lincoln ordered General Warner, with a detachment of militia from Massachusett's, to surprize and take Mount Independance. Colonel Brown, with Colonel Herrick's regiment of Rangers, and some militia and volunteers, were to cross the lake at the Narrows, and go through the woods and take Mount Defiance and the landing of Lake George ; those three places were to be attacked each in the gray of the same morning. Captain Ebenezer Allen, with his rangers, was to leave Colonels Brown and Herrick at a certain place, and take Mount Defiance, and then rejoin Brown and Herrick to take Ticondaroga, in conjunction with General Warner. The plan thus fixed they set off from Pawlet. General Warner moved so extremely cautious against Mount Independance, that he saved his own men, and hurt none of the enemy, and his expedition failed. Colonel Brown had many difficulties to encounter ; he had the lake to cross in the night, and fourteen miles to pass over rugged mountains, which he effected, and got within a few miles of the landing the day before the attack. Colonel Herrick took a few of his rangers, and went in sight of Lake George landing, and, from the mountains, made such discoveries as might be necessary ; and, on his return to rejoin the main body, stationed sentinels at certain distances, and rejoined Colonel Brown, after leaving this countersign, *three hoots of an owl*, on hearing which they were to answer ; Colonel Allen did the same on Mount Defiance, so that when they began their march, they were not in danger of missing their way through the darkness of the night, or being discovered by lights or noise, for they mimicked the owl so completely, that few of the men, who were not in the secret, had any mistrust. Colonel Brown surprized and took the landing, recovered many prisoners, and seized all their boats. Captain Allen had the most difficult task, though spirits equal to the undertaking. Mount Defiance garrison was on the top of a

high

high and rough mountain that overlooked Ticondaroga and Mount Independance, and had but one cut way to ascend to it, and that was well guarded. Allen and his men scaled the craggy rocks with much danger, and nearly reached the summit, when they found a clift they could not climb in the ordinary way; therefore Allen ordered a man to stoop, and he stepped on his back, and in that way ascended, but found that when he was up he could only secret about eight men, until they must come out in sight of, and close to the parade, where were several cannon, and the garrison, alarmed in consequence of the firing at the landing at Lake George. He commenced the desperate assault with an hideous yell, and, to use his own expression, *his men came after him like a stream of hornets to the charge,* which terrified most of the garrison, yet one man was bold enough to attempt to fire off a field-piece at the assailants; Allen having discharged his musket, cried out to his men, *Kill the gunner, Godd——n him!* at which the gun-ner turned from the field-piece, and ran off with the match in his hand. Allen and his men were soon in possession of the parade and garrison. Such men as were not killed or wounded, ran down the cut way towards Ticondaroga, and were taken by Major Wait and a party under him, stationed at the bridge for that purpose. Captain Allen had never discharged a cannon, but he levelled and fired a shot at the barrack on Mount Defiance, which killed one man; then, by a few shot, drove a ship in the lake from her moorings, and proclaimed himself Commandant of Mount Defiance. Colonel Brown, after his successes at Lake George landing, attempted to take Diamond Island, in Lake George, but without success; he, however, destroyed the boats at the landing, took a store of goods under the walls of Ticondaroga, put his booty into some boats he seized on Lake Champlain, and returned to Skeensboro' on his way back.

About this time General Schuyler was superceded, and General Gates took the command of the northern army. This change inspired the militia of New England with hope and confidence, and greatly cheared the drooping spirits of the army; and the militia of the neighbouring States, encouraged by the late successes of Generals Starks, Colonel Willet, &c. turned out with alacrity to assist General Gates.

The compliment paid to the troops of Vermont by General Burgoyne, in his letter to Lord George Germain, a little before his capitulation, was to this effect, viz. That the district of the New Hampshire grants, a wilderness, little known in the last war, now abounds with the most active, rebellious, and hardy race of

106

107

of men on the continent, who hang like a gathering storm ready
to burst on my left.

By the united forces of America, on the plains of Saratoga, was
witnessed the surrender of a British army, which was soon spread
through America and Europe, and sealed the alliance between
France and the United States of America, and secured to them
independence, further guaranteed by the combined forces of the
two nations in 1781, at York town, in Virginia, where Lord
Cornwallis and his army were obliged to surrender themselves
prisoners of *war*. After this digression, it is proper to return to
the northern army. Soon after the convention at Saratoga, the
garrisons of Ticondaroga, Mount Independance, and some other
places on Lake Champlain, were demolished by the British troops,
who retired into Canada for winter quarters, but they were followed by Colonel Herrick's rangers, and overtaken at Gilliland's
Creek, where they took a number of prisoners, horses, and some
baggage.

Now many of the citizens of Vermont returned to their habitations. The Council of Safety again paid attention to the constitution, and made a preamble, stating the reasons why the citizens
108 had rejected all connections with New York; but as there
was not time, before the day assigned for the election, to
print and publish the constitution, therefore the Convention was
summoned to meet at Windsor, in December, 1777; they met, re-
vised the constitution, and appointed the first election to be on
the 12th day of March, 1778. One difficulty was discovered by
some members of the Convention, who concluded the best way to
evade it was, to keep it in as small a circle as possible; the difficulty was, to establish the constitution without the voice of the
people, further than was vested in the Convention by their credentials, that authorized them to form a constitution, but were
silent as to its ratification, and they had no ancient government to
predicate their claims upon; besides intestine divisions and different opinions prevailed among the people, and even in the Convention. To avoid discord, a large majority, in one instance, con-
formed to a minority, when deliberating on the articles of the
constitution. As the people seemed inclined for a popular government, the constitution was so made, and for the better satisfy-
ing those who might choose any difference in the form of government, and as circumstances or increasing knowledge might make
it necessary, a principle was established in the constitution, by
which legal means might be taken to alter or amend the constitution once in seven years, agreeable to the will of the majority of
the

109 the freemen of the State, which, if perpetuated, would
transmit to posterity the same privileges of choosing how
they would be governed, as the people of that day exercised from
the inherent right of nature, without revolution or bloodshed.
Had the constitution been then submitted to the consideration of
the people for their revision, amendment, and ratification, it is
very doubtful whether a majority would have confirmed it, considering the resolutions of Congress, and their influence at that time,
as well as the intrigues and expence of the provincial Congress of
New York, who endeavoured to divide and subdivide the people.
Under these circumstances the Convention appointed Ira Allen to
see the constitution printed and distributed before the election.
Mr. Allen returned from Hartford, in Connecticut, a few days before the time of the general election, with the constitution printed,
and dispersed it.   There was one (or more) in each town who
coveted the honour of being a member in the first general Assembly of the new State of Vermont.   It was, therefore, their interest to induce their friends to attend the meeting, and take the
freeman's oath.   This was done, and representatives were elected,
and attended the Assembly at Windsor, on the 12th of March,
1778, when and where the votes of the freeman for a Governor, a
Lieutenant Governor, 12 Counsellors, and a Treasurer, were sort-
ed and counted, and the persons who had the majority of votes
110 for the respective offices, were declared duly elected.*—
Thus the constitution of the State of Vermont was put in

* His Excellency Thomas Chittenden, Governor.
The Hon. Joseph Marsh, Lieutenant Governor.

Counsellors.

The Honourable Joseph Bowker,
     Jacob Bayley,
     Jonas Fay,
     Timothy Brownson,
     Peter Olcott,
     Paul Spooner,
     Benj. Carpenter,   Esquires.
     Jeremiah Clark,
     Ira Allen,
     Thomas Moredock,
     John Troop,
     Benjamin Emmonds,

Treasurer, Ira Allen, Esq ;

The Members of the first Assembly of Vermont, the public will excuse the Author for not inserting their names, as his memory is not
sufficient to retain them in due order in a foreign land.

                    force

force, and Bennington was the only town that objected against the constitution, for the want of a popular ratification of it. Only twenty-one freemen qualified in that town, who elected representatives for the first general Assembly, but as the people and the assembly approved of the constitution, which was subject to a revision and amendment every seven years, the Bennington objection died away, and universal content has prevailed in the State.

111 In June, 1778, Colonel Ethan Allen having been exchanged, arrived in Vermont, to the great joy of his family and friends, after enduring a cruel captivity of almost three years, and was soon after appointed to the command of the militia of the State. The General Assembly appointed the Governor and Council to be a Court of Sequestration, and invested them with power to confiscate the real and personal property of any citizen who had joined the enemies of the State, and to order the sale of the same for the use of the State. The situation of Vermont was peculiar: its enemies, besides the British at the north, were those of New York at the south, and also a number of people of good sense and large property in the south-east part, who had leagued with the junto of New York against the new State. In consequence of internal divisions, and to make government popular, it was thought good policy not to lay any taxes on the people, but to raise a sufficient revenue out of the property confiscated, and the ungranted lands. Hence it was found that those who joined the British were benefactors of the State, as they left their property to support a government they were striving to destroy. It is further to be observed, that not only the civil list was paid by the sale of the enemy's property, but new and firm friends were added to the government. While the States in New England were severely taxed to carry on the war, Vermont had no taxes to pay. This circumstance greatly promoted migration into Vermont, and those who came with that view, were staunch 112 friends to the new government, and added to its strength and consequence both at home and abroad. The Legislature appointed Ira Allen, Esq; Surveyor General, and ordered him to procure, by his advertisement, all the grants, patents, or charters of land in the State, given out by the late Governors of New Hampshire and New York, and made his office a register for those grants, and, to encourage the proprietors of those grants, they were to be recorded at the expence of the State, although there was little attention paid to those of New York. Governor Wentworth, of New Hampshire, having carried the colonial records to England, rendered this measure necessary, in order to discover what lands had been granted, and to find out the ungranted lands, which undoubtedly

edly

edly were the property of the State, and to be granted on such advantageous terms as would afford an immediate revenue to government, and prevent all kinds of taxes.

Since the acquiescence of the late government of New Hampshire to the change of jurisdiction in 1764, a good understanding subsisted between New Hampshire and the district of the New Hampshire grants; indeed, that State had gone further towards the admission of Vermont to sovereignty and independence than any other, as will appear from President Weare's letter of July, 1777, to Ira Allen, Secretary of the State of Vermont, announcing
113 the assistance that State was sending, under the command of General Starks, for the defence of the frontiers; the stile and expressions in his letter were addressed to Vermont as a new but sovereign free State. From these circumstances, it appeared that New Hampshire had virtually acknowledged the independence of Vermont, and it was expected that she would use her influence to have it acknowledged by Congress; but these prospects were soon clouded by the conduct of some people contiguous to Connecticut River, in New Hampshire, who attempting privately to concert measures to bring the seat of government to said river, called a Convention at Hanover to concert measures to unite all the New Hampshire grants in one entire State; to effect which, a pamphlet was printed in 1778, in which it was stated, that New Hampshire was granted as a province to John Mason, and to extend sixty miles from the sea, which formed the line called and known by the name of the Mason line; that the lands to the west of that were annexed to New Hampshire by force of royal authority, and the lands were granted in pursuance of instructions from the King and Privy Council; that the jurisdiction of New Hampshire, west of the Mason line, ceased with the power of the crown, as it was held by force of royal commission only; that therefore the people were at liberty to chuse what form of government they would establish, and they thought proper to unite with the people of the New Hampshire grants, west of Connecticut River, who were about
114 to establish a new State. These measures drew the attention of the people, so that a petition from sixteen towns (including Hanover and others on the east side of Connecticut River) was presented to the legislature of Vermont, at their first session, in March, 1778; in the course of said petition it was stated, that said sixteen towns were not connected with any State with respect to their internal police, and requested Vermont to receive them into union and confederation. The legislature was much perplexed with this petition; the most discerning men were apprehensive of difficulty from New Hampshire if they interfered with her internal

police

police; the dispute arose so high, that some members contiguous to Connecticut River threatened to withdraw from the legislature, and unite with the people east of the said river, and form a State. At length it was resolved, to refer said petition to the consideration of the freemen of the several towns, to accept or reject said petition, and to instruct their representatives accordingly; a majority were in favor of said sixteen towns, consequently, at the next session of the legislature, an act was passed, authorizing said sixteen towns to elect and send members to the legislature of Vermont at their next session; this also laid a foundation for more towns to unite as aforesaid.

The sixteen towns announced to the government of New Hampshire that they had withdrawn from their jurisdiction, and wished 115 to have a boundary line settled between them, and a friendly intercourse continued.

Meshak Weare, Esq., was then President of that State, who wrote to Thomas Chittenden, Esq., Governor of Vermont, reclaiming said sixteen towns, predicating on the established bounds of the late province of New Hampshire; that said towns were represented in the provincial Congress in 1775; on their applying to that government for arms, &c., on their receiving commissions, and acting as a part of the State of New Hampshire; that a minority claimed protection; that the State felt it a duty to afford it. He also wrote to the delegates of that State in Congress, urging them to procure the interference of Congress; therefore President Weare recommended to Governor Chittenden to use his influence to dissolve so dangerous a connection.

On the receipt of these dispatches Governor Chittenden convened the Council, who appointed General Ethan Allen to repair to Congress in quality of agent to make such statements as might be consistent, and to learn how the conduct of Vermont was viewed by that body. General Ethan Allen reported to the legislature in October, 1778, that the members of Congress were unanimously opposed to Vermont's extending jurisdiction across Connecticut River; that if she dissolved her unions, they generally appeared in favour of her independence. At this time ten of said 116 sixteen towns were represented in the legislature of Vermont, when it was proposed to form the towns that had united with that State into a county by themselves, which was rejected by this and some other votes. It appeared that the Assembly declined to do any thing more to extend their jurisdiction to the east of Connecticut River. The members from those towns withdrew from the Assembly, and were followed by the Lieutenant Governor

nor, three members of the Council, and fifteen members of the Assembly, who lived near Connecticut River. The object was, to break up the Assembly, as the constitution required two-thirds of the members elected to form a house for business, but there remained a quorum who proceeded to business. They referred the matter respecting said sixteen towns to the freemen to instruct their representatives; as the union was formed by the voice of the people, the legislature chose to dissolve it in the same way. Ira Allen, Esq., was appointed and instructed to repair to the court of New Hampshire, in order to settle any difficulties that might subsist in consequence of said sixteen towns; Mr. Allen attended the General Court of New Hampshire, stated the causes that had produced said union, and the embarrassments the legislature of Vermont laboured under; that it would be dissolved at the adjourned term in February, which appeared satisfactory to the General Court of that State. The dissenting members of the legislature convened by themselves, and invited all the towns on the New Hampshire grants, on both sides of Connecticut 117 River, to send members to form a convention at Cornish, on the 9th of December, 1778. When the convention met, they agreed to unite, without any regard to the boundary line established on the west bank of Connecticut River in 1764. The Convention then proceeded to make the following proposals to the Government of New Hampshire, viz.

" Either to agree with them on a divisional line, or to submit the dispute to Congress, or to arbitrators mutually chosen." If neither of these proposals should be accepted, and they could agree with New Hampshire upon a plan of government, they resolved further, " We will consent that the whole of the grants connect with New Hampshire, and become with them one entire state, as it was limited and bounded, before the settling of the said line in 1764." Until one of these proposals should be complied with, they resolved to trust in Providence, and defend themselves.* There were but eight towns from Vermont which were represented in this convention, and some of them declined to act in making any overtures to New Hampshire, to extend their jurisdiction over the state of Vermont. But the proceedings of the Convention served to discover to the whole body of the people what had been the 118 views of the leading men, in proposing the union of the sixteen towns from New Hampshire.: It was now manifest, that their whole aim had been to form a government, the center and seat of which should be upon Connecticut River. This would be

* Allen's Vindication, p. 32, 33.

effected

effected either by connecting a considerable part of New Hampshire with Vermont, or by breaking up the government of Vermont, and connecting the whole of it with New Hampshire; the one or the other of these measures they were earnest to effect, and either of them would probably have formed a state, the metropolis of which must have been upon the river which divides the two states.

On the meeting of the legislature of Vermont at Windsor, February 12, 1779, to get rid of a connexion which had . occasioned so much trouble and danger, the Assembly passed an act, dissolving the union of the sixteen towns in New Hampshire. Mr. Ira Allen was again appointed to wait on the General Assembly of New Hampshire, then stting at Exeter, with the act of dissolution, and to make such explanations respecting the whole transaction as might be conducive to a good understanding between the two states. After discharging the duties of his mission, and before he left Exeter, he found it was the intention of some members in the Assembly of New Hampshire to extend jurisdiction over the territory of Vermont, under the pretence of opposing the claim of New York, and the befriending the new State in Congress. Mr. 119 Ira Allen thanked them for their good intentions, and offered, as his opinion, that Vermont would receive more benefit by their disinterested vote in Congress than by being a party. Mr. Ira Allen discovered the true, though secret cause of this pretended friendship towards Vermont, by a conversation of Major Atkinson, a member from Portsmouth, with some other members in a coffee-house, in which he observed that "as the seat of government had been moved from Portsmouth to Exeter, and would soon be removed to Concord, the eastern members ought to contrive and sell the seat of government to the highest bidder, and so let it go to Connecticut River; and as Governor Wentworth and his Council had made fortunes by granting lands, we may do the like by extending our jurisdiction, and giving out grants of unlocated lands, which will be included in the new acquisition.".

This conversation evidently showed what measures would be adopted by the Court of New Hampshire, to extend their claim. Mr. Ira Allen prudently kept the matter a secret, until he returned to Vermont, when he informed the Governor and Council thereof, who failed not to make proper use of the hints. They kept the matter a secret also, and, at the next session of the legislature (which was previous to the meeting of the General Court of New Hampshire,) Mr. Ira Allen was again appointed to go and concert 120 measures with the general Court of New Hampshire, with instructions to settle a boundary line between said States, to
quiet

quiet the minds of the people on both sides of Connecticut river, and to make them easy under their respective Governments.

Mr. Ira Allen attended the Court of New Hampshire, and made his mission known, but found they were pursuing measures to extend their jurisdiction over Vermont, from pretended friendship, and to overturn the claim of New York then before Congress; after which the Legislators of New Hampshire pretended they would withdraw their claim, and urge Congress to admit Vermont to be a State, and to have a seat in that venerable body. Upon such ostensible reasoning, Mr. Ira Allen was advised, as agent of Vermont, to assent to the plan and claim of New Hampshire, and was assured that the interest of Vermont as a separate State from New Hampshire, was the pledged principle on which they acted. Mr. Allen expressed no doubts of their sincerity, but replied, that he was convinced that it would be the opinion of the Governor and Council of Vermont, that the highest act of friendship to be shewn by the Legislature of New Hampshire to the State of Vermont, would be, not to become a party in the dispute, but to use her influence and vote in Congress in favour of Vermont, and to unite their mutual endeavours in quieting the people settled on both sides of Connecticut River, and rendering them contented 121 under their respective States, by establishing a boundary line.

In the mean time Mr. Allen discovered the President's plan was, under pretence of friendship to Vermont, to lay before Congress a claim of jurisdiction over the State; and that New Hampshire would make interest to have Congress decide against New York in her favour, to settle a dispute, that otherwise might be injurious to the common cause of the United States. That when such decision was made in favour of New Hampshire, the people that had professed allegiance to New York, and those who had withdrawn from the Legislature of Vermont with their friends, would naturally be for uniting with New Hampshire. That the people contiguous to Connecticut River, would feel an interest in joining with New Hampshire, on account of the seat of Government coming there.

That a union with New Hampshire would secure the title of Lands under the New Hampshire Grants, in consequence of which those on the west side of the Green Mountains, &c. would follow the example of those contiguous to Connecticut river, rather than contend alone for independence.

That

That the State of New Hampshire would be benefited by the
122 unlocated lands in the district of Vermont, and that, if possible, Mr. Allen should be persuaded to consent to such a
claim.

That President Weare, supposing Mr. Allen unacquainted with
the real object of the plan, fell in company with, and in conversation advised him to give his consent to the claim, as the means to
defeat the claim of New York, and bring Vermont into a confederacy with the thirteen United States, as a proper acknowledgment of her great exertions in the common cause, as well as
to quiet the minds of the people, and to settle the discord subsisting on both sides of Connecticut river, and declared on his honour
that he had no secret design of overthrowing the present system
of Government adopted in Vermont, or of uniting that State to
New Hampshire, and called God to witness the truth of his assertions ; several members of the Council and Assembly then present,
declared themselves in like manner. Mr. Allen thanked them for
their good intentions, and told them his present instructions and
power did not authorize him to assent to their claim, which he
opposed, and thought it very strange that the Legislature of New
Hampshire should insist upon doing Vermont a favour, when her
agent thought and contended that it would be an injury ; he therefore requested in general Court, that the determination of the
matter be referred to their next session, that the opinion of the
Legislature of Vermont might be taken thereon. The question
was moved and carried by a majority.

123   This procrastination was essential to Vermont, as it tended
to unite the people contiguous to Connecticut river on the
west, which was necessary at the next election, and to counteract
the designs of the *Cornish* Convention, as well as to gain time to
guard against the ill effects of such a claim, if extended, and which
afterwards was accordingly done, so that the jurisdictional claim
of New Hampshire extended as before the year 1764, including
the whole of Vermont.

Accordingly that State put into Congress a claim to the whole
territory of Vermont. As New Hampshire had not the least pretence, upon any principle whatever, to make such a claim, it was
not doubted in Vermont, but that intrigues had been formed by
the leading men in those two States, to divide Vermont between
them. Massachusetts now interposed ; whether aiming to disap-
point the views of New Hampshire and New York, or in earnest
to

to secure a part of the controverted lands, that State also put in a claim to a large part of Vermont.

While these controversies had been carried on with New Hampshire, the debate with New York had not at all subsided.   In a letter of July 7th, 1778, Mr. *Clinton*, Governor of New York, wrote to one of his friends in Vermont, that he " would still, as on a former occasion, earnestly recommend a firm and prudent resistance to the drafting of men, raising taxes, and the exercise 124 of every act of Government, under the ideal Vermont State ; and in such towns where our friends are sufficiently powerful for the purpose, I would advise the entering into association, for the mutual defence of their persons and estates against this usurpation."*   In a letter of July 8th, he warmly urged Congress to come to some decision on their controversy with Vermont ; blamed the inhabitants for the violence of their proceedings, affirmed that it would soon bring on a civil war, and that all the grievances the people of Vermont had suffered, arose from the former Government of New York, and not from the present.†

In 1779, the controversy with New York bore a more hostile appearance.   There were several persons in the south-east part of the State, then called the county of Cumberland, by New York, who were attached to the authority of that State, and opposed the Government of Vermont.   To some of them Governor *Clinton* had given commissions.   They asserted that they had a regiment of about five hundred men ; and that a committee of the county was also opposed to the authority of Vermont.

In this situation of affairs, the friends of New York in Vermont 125 concluded something decisive was necessary and ought to be done, if the jurisdiction was retained by New York ; therefore, a Mr. Patterson, who bore a Colonel's commission under the Government of New York, wrote to Governor Clinton, May 5, 1779, for directions how to proceed, and advising the necessity of calling out the militia of Albany county to enforce obedience to the State of New York ; adding, that any information could be obtained respecting the proceedings of the disaffected to the Government of New York, by employing the enemies of the new State, to give information.‡

* Copy of a letter from Governor *Clinton*, to Pelatiah Fitch, Esq.
† Attested copy.
‡ Patterson's letter to Governor Clinton, of May 5, 1779 ; and Minot's petition of May 4, 1779.

In

In answer to this application, the Governor of New York recommended in general, firmness and prudence, and in no instance to acknowledge the authority of Vermont, unless where there was no alternative left between submission and inevitable ruin: He assured them, at the same time, that if any attempt was made by Vermont to reduce them by force of arms, he would instantly issue his orders to the militia, who were properly equipped, and who would be led against the enemies of the State, wherever they might happen to be.*

Alarmed with these prospects, Mr. *Clinton* wrote to the President of Congress, May the 18th, that matters were fast approaching to a very serious crisis, which nothing but the immediate interposition of Congress could possibly prevent; that he daily expected that he should be obliged to order out a force, for the defence of those who adhered to New York; that the wisdom of Congress would suggest to them, what would be the consequence of submitting the controversy, especially at that juncture, to the decision of the sword; but that justice, the faith of government, the peace and safety of society, would not permit them to continue any longer, passive spectators of the violence committed on their fellow Citizens.† These letters, and sundry other papers relating to the disputes with New Hampshire, were laid before Congress, May 29th, 1779, and were referred to a committee of the whole. On June 1st, Congress resolved, " that a committee be appointed to repair to the inhabitants of a certain district, known by the name of the New Hampshire Grants, and inquire into the reasons why they refuse to continue citizens of the respective States, which heretofore exercised jurisdiction over the said district. And that they take every prudent measure to promote an amicable settlement of all differences, and prevent divisions and animosities, so prejudicial to the United States. "‡

Governor Chittenden being duly informed of this, as well as of the intended preparations, took speedy and secret measures to counteract them. Allen marched with an armed force, and made prisoners of the Colonel and militia officers, who were acting under the authority of New York, but they were released without fine after a friendly admonition, as the object was to shew power and lenity at once, as the most effectual mode of uniting the inhabitants of Vermont in the cause of their own Government.

126

127

* Clinton's letter to S. Minot, of May 14, 1779.
† Clinton's letter to Congress, of May 18, 1779.
‡ *Journal of Congress*, June 1, 1779, p. 237.

Governor

Governor Clinton, on hearing that the officers had been taken, on
June 7th wrote again to Congress, informing them what had happened, disapproving of their measures, and particularly of the
appointment of a committee to confer with the inhabitants ; and
wishing their journey might be postponed, until the Legislature
of New York should be convened, and take the resolutions of
Congress under consideration.   On the 16th, Congress resolved
that the officers who had been thus restrained of their liberty ought
to be immediately liberated ;* and that their committee who were
appointed to confer with the inhabitants, should be directed to
make enquiry into the matters and things contained in Governor
Clinton's letters ; and that all further proceedings be postponed
until they should report.†

The taking of the civil and military officers, acting in the south-
cast part of Vermont, under New York, unhappily did not recon-
128 cile parties ; and the friends of New York in that district
gave out that they were not apprized of the designs of the
Green Mountain Boys, who would not again be able to do the like,
as Governor Clinton would in future take care and protect them.
Peace, order, and submission to the laws of Vermont were by no
means established, which occasioned many difficulties to arise
among the people, increased in consequence of their living mixed
together.   In some towns a majority was in favour of Vermont,
and a minority in favour of New York ; and in others it was *vice
versa ;* and it often happened that men of the most information
and property were in the minority ; in others a majority were in
favour of New York, while the minority represented them in the
Legislature of Vermont.

To establish Government in the minds of the people, and consolidate all parties, became necessary ; policy, armed with power and
lenity, were therefore resorted to, and a law was enacted, empower-
ing the Supreme Court to mulct or inflict corporeal punishment on
the opposers of the laws of Vermont, not exceeding *forty stripes*,
save one. Soon after this law had been made and promulgated, some
property was to be sold at vendue by an officer acting under the
laws and authority of Vermont, when some principal people, in
the interest of New York, met and opposed the officer in the execution of his duty ; pains were taken to find out the strength and

* It appears at this time, that Congress was not acquainted with the
generous conduct of the Government of Vermont to their prisoners.
† Journal of Congress, June 16, 1779, p. 259, 260.

situation

129 situation of the opposers, and the plan of a secret expedition
was accordingly laid ; warrants were issued against the opposers in the several towns in the county of Cumberland, (as
called by New York) who had been active in the interest of New
York ; and General Ethan Allen called out the militia in support
of the civil power of Vermont; the oppositionists, widely scat-
tered, were, notwithstanding, through the vigilance of the Green
Mountain Boys, all taken by virtue of warrants issued against
them, except one who was from home on a journey ; they were
brought to Westminster, and confined in the prison ; many of
them were Gentlemen of property and great respectability, and
being in the power of the officers of Government, were liable to
corporeal penishment, by laws they had never submitted or as-
sented to. This occasioned much conversation, and their friends
sought to raise the militia of New Hampshire to rescue them.

Matters became so serious, that General Bellows, of the New
Hampshire militia, wrote to Colonel Ira Allen on the subject, and
received an answer, *not to mind appearances, but to believe the
characters of the gentlemen would be preserved as well as that of
the State.* The delinquents were brought before the Court, and
acknowledged its jurisdiction ; they were ordered to pay each a
small fine, and dismissed. This ·lenient measure established the
power and laws of Vermont in the hearts of the people, and made
130 such an impression on the minds of the late prisoners, that
within two years they filled some of the first offices of that
State.

" Five Commissioners were appointed to repair to Vermont : Of
these but two, Dr. Witherspoon, and Mr. Atlee, attended. These
gentlemen repaired to Bennington in June, made many inquiries,
and had several conferences with the friends of Vermont, and with
others who were in the interest of New York. They proposed
several questions to the Governor of Vermont, to which he returned written answers. Their aim seems to have been, to bring
about a reconciliation between the parties. Upon their return they
made a report to Congress, July 13th ; but which evidently de-
noted, that no part of the business on which they were sent, had
been effected*."

Four different claims were now before Congress, to the same
tract of country ; and the controversy had become so intricate and
warm, that very serious consequences were justly to be feared.

* Account of the proceedings of Mr. Witherspoon, and Mr. Atlee.

It

It became necessary for Congress to interpose ; and as all parties had appealed to that body, they could no longer avoid coming to some resolutions upon a matter which seemed essentially to concern the union of the States. Accordingly, on September 24, 1779, Congress, among other resolves, passed the following :

131

" Resolved unanimously, That it be, and hereby is most earnestly recommended, to the States of New Hampshire, Massachusett's Bay, and New York, forthwith to pass laws, expressly authorizing Congress to hear and determine all differences between them, relative to their respective boundaries.

" Resolved unanimously, That Congress will, on the first day of February next, proceed without delay, to hear and examine into the disputes and differences relative to jurisdiction aforesaid, between the said three States respectively, or such of them as shall pass the laws beforementioned, on the one part, and the people of the district aforesaid, who claim to be a separate jurisdiction on the other, and after a full and fair hearing, will decide and determine the same according to equity.

" Resolved unanimously, That it is the duty of the people of the district aforesaid, who deny the jurisdiction of all the aforenamed States, to abstain, in the mean time, from exercising any power over any of the inhabitants of the said district, who profess themselves to be citizens of, or to owe allegiance to any or either of the said States, but that none of the towns, either on the east or west side of Connecticut River, be considered as included within the said district, but such as have hitherto actually joined in denying the jurisdiction of either of said States, and have assumed a separate jurisdiction, which they call the State of Vermont.—And further, that in the opinion of Congress, the said three States aforenamed, ought in the mean time to suspend executing their laws over any of the inhabitants of the said district, except such of them, as shall profess allegiance to, and confess the jurisdiction of the same respectively.

132

" Resolved unanimously, That in the opinion of Congress, no unappropriated lands or estates, which are or may be adjudged forfeited, or confiscated, lying in said district, ought, until the final decision of Congress in the premises, to be granted or sold."*

* Journal of Congress, September 24, 1779,

These

These resolves of Congress arrived in Vermont a little time before the session of the General Assembly in October, 1779. The influence of Congress at that time was great, being considered as the pillar of liberty; and their advice was deemed a law; the friends of New York exulted, and doubled their exertions against Vermont: When the Assembly convened, nine-tenths were for suspending the sale of confiscated property, and the granting of lands till after the 1st of Februray, the time assigned by Congress to examine into the disputes and differences, but a few saw the design of the New York junto was to cut off the resources, and to 133 prevent migrations of persons from other States, who became internal friends; they saw also, if they submitted to one decree of Congress against the interest of Vermont, the same influence of the junto would prevail on Congress to annihilate the existence of Vermont as a State. Moreover, they knew themselves not to be under the controul of Congress, having no representative in that body; and finally, by the union of the States, Congress was not authorized to interfere with the internal police of any State in the union; how then could they interfere with Vermont, which was out of the union? After fourteen days consideration, the Governor, Council, and General Assembly, in Grand Committee, recommended to the Legislature to grant the whole of their unlocated lands, and sell their confiscated estates, or such parts as might be thought proper; which recommendation was approved by unanimous resolves of the General Assembly, and copies thereof sent to Congress.

The Legislature next proceeded to establish a form of a charter, and the manner that should be used in granting lands. Each township was to be six miles square, and to be granted in seventy shares, to specific names, inserted in the charter. Five of those shares were for public use, (viz.) *one* right for the use of a seminary or college within the State, *one* right for the use and benefit of the first settled Minister of the Gospel in the township, *one* right for the use and support of the ministry in the town for ever, *one* right for the use and support of county grammar-schools through- 134 out the State, and *one* right for the use and support of an English school or schools in the township for ever. Under these regulations, several charters were issued at this session of the Legislature, regardless of the resolves of Congress. To discover the several interests and dispositions of each State south of New York, respecting the interest and independence of Vermont, and to shew the consequence of that State heretofore in the common cause, as well as to demonstrate the natural and divine right the people have to form a Government for themselves, the General
Assembly

Assembly appointed Ira Allen, Esq. to attend the Legislatures of
New Jersey, Pennsylvania, Delaware, Maryland, and other States,
if time permitted, before the 1st of February, 1780, and on that
day to be at Philadelphia, and join Jonas Fay, Moses Robinson,
and Stephen R. Bradley, as a committee, by the Assembly of Vermont appointed to wait on Congress, and shew the just claim the
State had to be independent, and to hold the lands under New
Hampshire Grants.

Mr. Allen, according to his appointment, attended the Legislatures of the fore-named States, and distributed sundry pamphlets
written in vindication of the claims and doings of Vermont. Many
questions arose respecting the local interest of Vermont, by a
junction with the other States, and their views, touching the unlocated lands, and the confiscated property of the royalists. It is
135 to be observed, that a question subsisted in Congress, respecting the unappropriated lands, and the property of the
loyalists, who had joined the enemy against the independence of
the United States. These four States were of opinion that all
property wrested from the king of Great Britain and his adherents,
by the efforts of the people of the United States, ought to be disposed of for defraying the expences of the war, and not for the
emolument of any one State in which it was situated or was
claimed. These States (Pennsylvania excepted) had no claims
of consequence in the west; neither had Vermont; therefore,
upon a similar interest, and on the assurance of Mr. Allen, that if
Vermont was admitted to a seat in Congress, she would adhere to
those principles, they seemed to wish to favour the interest of Vermont. Mr. Allen urged, that an account of the lands granted and
confiscated in Vermont, should be accounted for as a small part
of their unlocated lands and confiscated estates throughout the
United States; that as partners in common and new beginners, it
was necessary to make use of a part of their share for the common
good, being very much exposed to the common enemy, from an
extensive frontier contiguous to Champlain and Canada, and from
whence eruptions might easily be made into the State of New
York, and the New England States, in case of rendering Vermont
of no importance in the union; further, that the disposal of such
lands and property furnished money to defray the expences in part
136 of the war, helped to alleviate, in a considerable degree, the
burthens of the people, and to strengthen the frontiers against
the common enemy. These reasons, with the political consequence
of Vermont in the capture of Ticondaroga, Crown Point, &c. and
the cutting off the first wing of General Burgoyne's army, operated
in a two-fold degree, and had a salutary effect on Congress. On
the

the 1st of February, 1780, the Commissioners from Vermont met at Philadelphia, but nothing conclusive was done, and the agents returned home, after having made official offers in behalf of the the State, to bear full and just proportion of the expences of the war, on their being admitted to a seat in Congress.

In the mean time the Governor and Council published an appeal to the candid and impartial world,* in which they declare " that they could not view themselves as holden, either in the sight of God or man, to submit to the execution of a plan, which they had reason to believe was commenced by neighbouring States : That the liberties and privileges of the State of Vermont, by said resolutions, are to be suspended upon the arbitrament and final determination of Congress, when, in their opinion, they were things too sacred ever to be arbitrated upon at all ; and what they were 137 bound to defend, at every risk : That the Congress of the United States had no right to intermeddle in the internal police and government of Vermont : That the State existed independent of any of the thirteen United States, and was not accountable to them, or to their representatives, for liberty, the gift of the beneficent Creator : That the State of Vermont was not represented in Congress, and could not submit to resolutions passed without their consent, or even knowledge, and which put every thing that was valuable to them, at stake : That there appeared a manifest inequality, not to say predetermination, that Congress should request of their constituents power to judge and determine in the cause, and never ask the consent of thousands, whose all was at stake : They also declared that they were, and ever had been, ready to bear their proportion of the burden and expence of the war with Great Britain, from its first commencement, whenever they were admitted into the union with the other States : But they were not so lost to all sense, and honour, that after four years war with Britain, in which they had expended so much blood and treasure, that they should now give up every thing worth fighting for, the right of making their own laws, and choosing their own form of government, to the arbitrament and determination of any man, or body of men, under heaven."

On the 21st of March, 1780, it was ordered by Congress that the matter be postponed, nine States, (exclusive of those who 138 were parties in the question) not being represented.† On June 2d, Congress resolved that the proceedings of the people of the

* Drawn up by Stephen R. Bradley, Esq. published December 10, 1779.
† Journal of Congress, March 21, 1780, p. 47, 49.

New

New Hampshire Grants were highly unwarranable, and subversive of the peace and welfare of the United States; and that they be strictly required to forbear from any acts of authority, civil or military, over those of the people who professed allegiance to other States: And on June the 9th, they resolved to defer the matter to the second Tuesday in September.* Upon the receipt of these resolves, the Governor of Vermont, by the advice of his Council, replied, that "however Congress might view those resolutions, they were considered by the people of Vermont as being in their nature subversive of the natural right which they had to liberty and independence, as well as incompatible with the principles on which Congress grounded their own right to independence, and had a natural and direct tendency to endanger the liberties of America; that Vermont being a free and independent State, had denied the authority of Congress to judge of their jurisdiction; that as they were not included in the thirteen United States, if necessitated to it, they were at liberty to offer or accept terms of cessation of hostilities with Great Britain, without the approbation of any other man, or body of men; for, on proviso that neither Congress, nor the Legislatures of those States which
139 they represent, will support Vermont in her independence, but devote her to the usurped government of any other power, she had not the most distant motive to continue hostilities with Great Britain, and maintain an important frontier, for the benefit of the United States, and for no other reward than the ungrateful one, of being enslaved by them; but notwithstanding the usurpations and injustice of neighbouring governments towards Vermont, and the late resolutions of Congress, from a principle of virtue, and close attachment to the cause of liberty, as well as from a thorough examination of their own policy, they were induced once more to offer union with the United States of America, of which Congress were the legal representative body."†

In August, 1780, Ira Allen and Stephen Bradley, Esquires, attended Congress, as agents from Vermont, in order to be prepared for the second Tuesday in September (to which time Congress had referred the determination of the cause of Vermont.) The people in the south-east part of the State who professed allegiance to the state of New York, sent their agent, Luke Knowlton, Esq; to attend Congress; and the people in the north-east part of the State, who were, in opinion and politics, with the revolting members of the Legislature of Vermont in 1778, also sent their agent, Peter

* Journal of Congress, June 9th, 1780, p. 81, 82, 84.

† Governor Chittenden's letter to Congress, of July 25th, 1780.

Olcott,

Olcott, Esq; to Congress; thus, to that body, all parties appeared
140 to be represented.   The agents of Vermont had frequent interviews with the members of Congress, in particular those
from New York, with whom they spent several evenings in the
most sociable manner.   Very different views and objects seemed
to be pursued by all parties ; indeed, all parties seemed determined to carry their point.   Therefore, to gain as great an advantage as possible, the agents of Vermont requested in writing, that
when any debates came before Congress which might affect the
rights, the sovereignty, or independence of the State of Vermont,
they might be present.   On this request, the opponents to Vermont
took courage, supposing that by getting the agents to attend in
Congress, they would make some remarks on the evidence adduced
against the independence of Vermont, or, in some way, put it in
the power of that body to consider the cause to them submitted by
the agents of Vermont.

On the 19th of September, 1780, they received a notification to
attend Congress, to hear the question respecting the jurisdiction
of the New Hampshire Grants.   The claims of New Hampshire
and New York were put in, and both of these States plead that
Vermont had no pretensions to independence, but belonged to
them.   The agents of Vermont, though present, were not considered or treated by Congress as the agents or representatives of any
State or people invested with legislative authority.   Part of two
141 days were spent in hearing the evidence exhibited by New
York, to shew that the people on the New Hampshire Grants
belonged to, and of right were under the authority and jurisdiction of New York, and therefore had no right to a separate independent jurisdiction.   A day being assigned to hear the claim and
evidence of New Hampshire, during this time the Agents of Vermont retained minutes of the proceedings of Congress, and of the
evidence exhibited by the Agents of New York, that they might
the better be prepared to remonstrate against them, as they had
no idea of submitting the independence of Vermont to the arbitrament of Congress, or even of speaking on the matter in Congress, or of objecting in any way to the evidence adduced against
Vermont, however irregular or provoking.   The principles upon
which the Agents of Vermont went, were to remain quiet, let the
business be conducted as it would : the worse, the more advantage
they would have in remonstrating ; they concluded it not advisable
to attend and hear the claim and evidence of New Hampshire
when it was taken up by Congress, therefore sent in their remonstrance to that body, and declined attending.   Mr. Thompson,
Secretary, (of Congress) called on and urged them to attend,·
which

which they refused; he then requested to know what report he should return to Congress; when he received for answer, *that while Congress sat as a Court of Judicatory, authorized by the claiming States ex parte, and Vermont was not put on an equal footing, they should not again darken the doors of Congress;* the remonstrance was as follows.

142

" To the Honourable C o n g r e s s of the U n i t e d S t a t e s of N o r t h A m e r i c a.

" The remonstrance of Ira Allen and Stephen R. Bradley, Commissioners from the free and independent State of Vermont, appointed for the time being to attend on Congress.

" With pleasure they embrace this first opportunity to testify their thanks for the personal honour done them by Congress, in giving them an attendance, though in a private capacity, with their honourable body: At the same time they lament the necessity which obliges them to say, they can no longer sit as idle spectators, without betraying the trust reposed in them, and doing violence to their feelings, to see partial modes pursued, plans adopted, ex parte evidence exhibited, which derives all its authority from the attestation of the party ; passages of writings selected giving very false representations of facts, to answer no other end but to prejudice your honourable body against the *State of Vermont;* thereby to intrigue and baffle a brave and meritorious people out of their rights and liberties. We can easily conceive the Secretary's office of the State of New York may be converted into an inexhaustible source to furnish evidence to answer their purpose in the present dispute.

143

" Needless would it be for us to inform Congress, that by the mode of trial now adopted, the State of Vermont can have no hearing without denying itself: And to close with those resolutions, which we conceive our enemies have extorted from your honourable body, and on which the trial is now placed, would be, in fact, taking upon ourselves that humility and self abasement, as to lose our political life, in order to find it.

" We believe the wisdom of Congress sufficient to point out, that pursuing the present mode, is deviating from every principle of the laws of nature, or nations: For if the dispute is between the States claiming on the one part, and the State of Vermont on the other, whether the latter be a State *de jure*, or an indpendent jurisdiction

jurisdiction *de facto*, they ought to be considered in the course of the dispute, until the powers interposing have determined whether the latter be an independent jurisdiction *de jure ;* if not they of course ought to annihilate the jurisdiction *de facto ;* but to annihilate the State *de facto*, in the first place, is summarily ending the dispute ; to deny the latter any independent jurisdiction *de facto*, is to deny there is any longer parties in the dispute.

144 " Again, we conceive the means connected with the end, and upon no principle whatever can we justify, that either part should establish the modus, or rules to be pursued in determining disputes, without confounding every idea of right and wrong. In the present case, on the one part might the end as justly have been established as the way and means to effect the end.

" We are far from being willing those brave and strenuous efforts made by the State of Vermont, in the controversy with Great Britain, should be buried by our grasping adversaries (thirsting after domination and prey) in the specious pretext of riotously assuming Government ; and we thereby lose all credit for the men and money we have expended.

" Thus, while we are necessitated to remonstrate against the proceedings of Congress on the present mode, we are willing, at the same time, any equitable enquiry should be made, the State of Vermont being allowed equal privileges with the other States in the dispute.

" And that the State of Vermont might stand justified to your honourable body, and to the world, both as to her present and future conduct, we are induced, as well from principles of attachment to the American cause, as a regard we have for peace 145 and harmony among the states of America now at war with Great Britain, to make the following proposals, viz.

" 1st. That the State of Vermont will, as soon as may be, forward to the Secretary of Congress, an attested return of all male persons, liable to do duty agreeable to a militia act heretofore exhibited to Congress in a code of laws, entitled, " The Laws of Vermont ;" and the State of Vermont shall, for and during the present war with Great Britain, from year to year, furnish an equal number of troops in the field, in proportion to their numbers, as Congress shall estimate the quotas of the several United States, in proportion to their numbers ; which troops shall be clothed, quartered, and paid by the State of Vermont. And, at the close of of the war, the dispute shall be equitably settled by the mediation of sovereign powers; and nothing herein contained, shall be construed to take away the right any of the United States claim to have in or over the State of Vermont: Or

" 2dly, We are willing to agree upon some one or more of the Legislatures of the disinterested States to interpose as mediators, and settle the dispute : Or

" 3dly, We are willing Congress, being possessed of sovereignty, should interpose to prevent the effusion of human blood ; at the same time, we reprobate every idea of Congress sitting as a Court of Judicature, to determine the dispute, by virtue of authority given them by the act or acts of the State or States that make but one party.

146

" It gives us pungent grief that such an important cause at this juncture of affairs, on which our *all* depends, should be forced on by any gentlemen professing themselves friends to the cause of America, with such vehemence and spirit as appears on the part of the State of New York: And shall only add, that if the matter be thus pursued, we stand ready to appeal to God and the world, who must be accountable for the awful consequences that may ensue.

" *Done at Philadelphia, this 22d day*
   of September, A. D. 1780.

" IRA ALLEN,
" STEPHEN R. BRADLEY."

Congress having heard the evidence on the part of New Hampshire, on the 27th of September, resolved that the further consideration of the subject should be postponed.

A plan was then laid between two persons at Philadelphia, to unite all parties in Vermont, in a way that would be honourable to those who had been in favour of New York, and said sixteen towns, that would also justify the Legislature of Vermont, to effect which, measures were taken to induce some of the western members of the Council and Assembly of New Hampshire, who had exerted themselves to extend the jurisdictional claim of New Hampshire over the territory of Vermont, to write circular letters to convene a Convention at Walpoole, which met in December

147

ber

ber, 1780;[1] after some deliberation they issued new writs for a full Convention of Representatives from all the towns, granted by New Hampshire, on both sides of the Connecticut river, and adjourned that Convention to the 16th of January, 1781, to meet in Charlestown, upon information of which, the Governor and Council appointed Colonel Ira Allen to repair to Charlestown to meet that Convention, and to take such measures as his prudence should dictate, and which might be conducive to the interest of the State. Mr. Allen took credentials from Sunderland, as a member, to meet the Convention, from that town, agreeable to invitation; before he arrived, the Convention had been in session two days, and had appointed a Committee to state the business of their meeting. Forty-three towns were represented in the Convention; twelve of those representatives were members of the Council and Assembly of New Hampshire. Mr. Allen did not take a seat as a member of the Convention, nor produce his credentials; at length the Committee reported to unite all the New Hampshire grants to New Hampshire, which was adopted by a great majority, and went in fact to annihilate the State of Vermont. Mr. Allen informed some confidential persons, that the Governor, Council, 148 and some other leading characters, on the west side of the Green Mountains, were for extending their claim of jurisdiction to the Mason line; and that if the Convention would take proper measures the Legislature of Vermont would extend their claim at their adjourned term in February, 1781; and that he was authorized to give such assurance.

A motion was made and carried, to consider the report, and recommit it to the committee, to be corrected and fitted for the press, as it would be a matter of public notoriety, and to lay it again before the Convention next morning. The friends of New Hampshire were much pleased with their success, and well enjoyed the night; but the scene changed the next morning, and the committee reversed their report, and reported to unite all the territory of New Hampshire, west of Mason's east line, extending to Connecticut river, with the State of Vermont; and which report was accepted by a great majority of the Convention, it being principally opposed by twelve members of the Council and Assembly of New Hampshire, who, thereupon, withdrew to remonstrate against the proceeding.

This bare-faced conduct of the members of the Legislature disclosed their intention at once, and furnished Vermont with fair

---

[1] [This Convention met November 16th, 1780. *Slade*, p. 126–127.]

pretensions

pretensions to extend her jurisdiction on grounds of similar policy and self-preservation.

149   The Convention then appointed a Committee to confer with the Legislature of Vermont at their next term, and adjourned to meet at Cornish (only three miles from Windsor, the place of session of the Legislature of Vermont, agreeable to adjournment) on the same day with them.

On February 10th, the Committee informed the Assembly, then sitting at Windsor, that " the Convention of the New Hampshire towns was desirous of being united with Vermont, in one separate independent Government, upon such principles as should be mutually thought the most equitable and beneficial to the whole." In consequence of this application, the Legislature resolved, on February 14th, that " in order to quiet the present disturbances on the two sides of the river (Connecticut) and the better to enable the inhabitants on the two sides of said river to defend their frontier, the Legislature of this State do lay a *jurisdictional claim* to all the lands whatever, east of Connecticut river, north of Massachusetts, west of the Mason line, and south of latitude 45° ; and that they do not exercise jurisdiction for the time being." The Convention of the New Hampshire towns was then sitting at Cornish, on the opposite side of the river ; and on February 22d, the articles of union were agreed upon, and confirmed ; nevertheless, the right of dissolving the union of the district was retained by the State of Vermont.

150   The first information that the people of Vermont heard, that the British Generals in America thought to avail themselves of an advantage in the disputes that subsisted between the claiming States and Congress, on the one part, and Vermont on the other, was contained in a letter from Colonel Beverley Robinson, dated New York, March 30th, 1780, directed to Colonel Ethan Allen, which was delivered to him in July in the street in Arlington. Mr. Allen perused the letter, then told the bearer that he should consider of it, and that he might return.

Colonel Robinson begins his letter thus: " I am now undertaking a task, which I hope you will receive with the same good intention that inclines me to make it. I have often been informed that you, and most of the inhabitants of Vermont, are opposed to the wild and chimerical scheme of the Americans, in attempting to separate this continent from Great Britain, and to establish an independent state of their own ; and that you would willingly assist

sist in uniting America again to Great Britain, and restoring that happy constitution we have so wantonly and unadvisedly destroyed. If I have been rightly informed, and these should be your sentiments and inclination, I beg you will communicate to me, without reserve, whatever proposals you would wish to make to the Commander in Chief; and I hereby promise that I will faithfully lay them before him, acording to your directions, and 151 flatter myself I can do it to as good effect as any person whatever. I can make no proposals to you, until I know your sentiments, but think upon your taking an active part, and embodying the inhabitants of Vermont in favour of the crown of England, to act as the Commander in Chief shall direct, that you may obtain a separate government, under the King and constitution of England, and the men, formed into regiments under such officers as you shall recommend, be on the same footing as all the provincial corps are. If you should think proper to send a friend of your own here with proposals to the General, he shall be protected, and well treated here, and allowed to return whenever he pleases."

General Allen immediately communicated the contents of it to the Governor and some confidential persons, who agreed in opinion that it was best not to return any answer; but it was agreed, that in consequence of application to the Governor of the friends of some persons that had been taken at Royaltown, who were prisoners in Canada, that the Governor should address a letter to the Commander in Chief, General Haldiman, on the subject of a cartel for the exchange of prisoners, and send a flag with it to the first British ship stationed on the Lake, which was accomplished; in October the British appeared in great force on the Lake; such was the alarm, that the Legislature, who were then in session at 152 Bennington, adjourned, and many of its members took arms, and repaired to the frontiers.

General Ethan Allen received a flag from Major Carlton, with an answer to Governor Chittenden's letter, also proposing a truce with Vermont, for the settlement of a cartel for the exchange of prisoners. General Allen agreed to the truce, on condition that the frontiers of New York should be included to Hudson's River. This additional territory produced some altercation; for, on the part of Major Carlton, it disappointed his expedition; on the part of General Allen, it would have been exposing Vermont to many difficulties, had her General consented to a truce, and left the frontiers of a neighbouring State exposed. However, in consideration of future prospects, General Allen's proposition was admitted

mitted, and a truce was settled, including the frontiers of the State of New York to Hudson's River. This stipulation was not publicly known; the militia of Vermont were immediately disbanded, and permitted to return home. A few days then were very material to the farmer in putting his winter wheat into the ground. The militia of the district to Hudson's River were also on their frontiers, and were much surprised to find that the militia of Vermont were returning home, and that the British troops were retiring to Canada to winter quarters. It was further agreed, that commissioners should meet on the subject of said cartel. Justus Sherwood, and George Smith, Esquires, were ap-
153 pointed on the part of the British, Colonel Ira Allen and Major Joseph Fay on the part of Vermont, who met, and all agreed to go into Canada together. When they arrived at East Bay, an early and severe frost had obstructed their way in consequence of the ice. While their men were breaking through the ice, much political conversation and exhibits of papers took place. After contending several days with the elements, it was agreed that the British commissioners should take the stores of both parties, and make their way into Canada, and that Allen and Fay should return to Vermont, and to see that commissioners should repair to Canada as soon as circumstances would admit. In the winter, the honourable Jonas Fay, Esq. was commissioned to accomplish the same object, and went as far as Split Rock, on Lake Champlain, where he found the ice insufficient, and with difficulty got off, and made his return.

On February 2, 1781, Colonel Robinson wrote again to General Ethan Allen, inclosing a copy of the former, in which he writes— " The frequent accounts we have had for three months past, from your part of the country, confirms me in the opinion I had of your inclination to join the King's cause, and to assist in restoring America to her former peaceable and happy constitution. This induces me to make another trial, in sending this to you; especially as I can now write with more authority, and assure you, that you may obtain the terms mentioned in the above letter,
154 provided you and the people of Vermont take a decisive and active part with us."* He requests an answer, and that some method might be pointed out for carrying on a correspondence for the future, and information in what manner the people of Vermont could be the most serviceable to the British government, " either by acting with the northern army, or to meet and join an army from New York."

* Copy of Robinson's letter of Feb. 2, 1781, to E. Allen.

Allen

Allen returned no answer to either of these lettess; but on March 9th, 1781, inclosed them in a letter to Congress. In his letter to that body, he made observations, justifying Vermont in asserting her right to independence; in which he observed, conscious of his own integrity, and sensible that his activity and sufferings in the cause of his country were known to all America— " I am confident that Congress will not dispute my sincere attachment to the cause of my country, though I do not hesitate to say, I am fully grounded in opinion that Vermont has an indubitable right to agree on terms of a cessation of hostilities with Great Britain, provided the United States persist in rejecting her application for an union with them: for Vermont, of all people would be the most miserable, were she obliged to defend the independence of the United claiming States, and they, at the same time, at full liberty to overturn, and ruin the independence of Vermont. 155 I am persuaded, when Congress consider the circumstances of this state, they will be more surprized that I have transmitted them the inclosed letters, than that I have kept them in custody so long; for I am as resolutely determined to defend the independence of Vermont, as Congress are that of the United States; and rather than fail, will retire with hardy Green Mountain Boys, into the desolate caverns of the mountains, and wage war with human nature at large."

In October, 1780, General Ethan Allen, by his truce with the British at Castleton, included all the territory laying between Vermont and the Hudson's River. The people in that district felt grateful for such unexpected protection from a powerful invading army, and having recently suffered so much from General Burgoyne's army, they could more readily realize the benefits than account for the cause. It appeared to them like a text of scripture, " And the Lord put a hook in their nose, and turned them about the way they came." The people of this district had great confidence in General Allen, many of whom were personally acquainted with him when he commanded the Green Mountain Boys against the late colony of New York; they knew of his taking Ticondaroga, Crown Point, &c. as well as of his long and severe captivity, from which, and knowing the decided part the people 156 of Vermont had generally taken in the common cause of America, those of this description would unite with Vermont for common defence. Those friendly to the British interest and politics were influenced by an idea that Vermont was about to join Great Britain; others supposed that she did not mean to act for either Congress or Great Britain, which, with the assurance of some leading people in Vermont, that the Legislature would extend

tend their jurisdiction over them, induced a number of the inhabitants to present a petition to the assembly of Vermont, praying protection, and to be received into union.

Accordingly, on February 14th, it was resolved, " that the Legislature of this State do lay a jurisdictional claim to all the land situate north of the north line of the State of Massachusett's, and extending the same to Hudson's River, east of the center of the deepest channel of said river, to the head thereof; from thence east of a north line, being extended to latitude 45°; and south of the same line, including all the lands and waters to the place where this State now exercise jurisdiction.—And not to exercise jurisdiction for the time being."*

Thus, while New Hampshire and New York were extending their claims over the whole territory of Vermont, Vermont 157 adopted the same policy; and in conformity to the petition of the inhabitants, extended her claim over a large part of the territory of both these States.

Great success attended this policy; Not only the sixteen towns in New Hampshire which had formerly joined, but those in Vermont, which had been disaffected upon the dissolution of the former union, and those that had been attached to New York, immediately joined in the measure. Most of the towns in the adjacent counties of Cheshire, and Grafton, in New Hampshire, declared for the union: And at a session of the Assembly of Vermont in April, thirty-five towns in the western parts of New Hampshire were represented.—The adjacent settlements in New York generally embraced the same measures, and several petitions were received from their inhabitants at this session of the Assembly, requesting the Legislature of Vermont to exercise jurisdiction over them without any further delay. A Committee was appointed by the Assembly, to confer with a Convention of those districts; and on May 15th, articles of union were agreed to, by the representatives of twelve districts in New York, and the Committee from Vermont. On the 16th of June, these articles were confirmed by the Legislature, and representatives from ten of the districts took their seats in the Assembly of Vermont.†

158 The Legislature of Vermont, the better to restore peace, order, and submission to its government, to consolidate the affections of the people, and add to her internal strength at the

* Journal of the Assembly of Vermont, Vol. I. Feb. 14, 1781.
† Journal of the Assembly of Vermont, Vol. I. June 16, 1781.

time

time of extending her jurisdictional claims as aforesaid, wisely passed a general act of amnesty in favour of all those who had opposed her laws. This liberal act of lenity had its desired effect, and all opposition within the ancient territory of Vermont ceased for a considerable time.

At the time of projecting these unions, and laying the basis for the first in Philadelphia, which also united the people contiguous to Connecticut River, the State of Vermont was in a forlorn situation, torn by intestine divisions and the intrigues of her enemies in Congress; all the cannon, nay, every spade and pickaxe taken by her valiant sons at Ticondaroga and Crown Point, were removed out of the State to Fort George, together with Colonel Warner's regiment, raised in and for the protection of Vermont, but put into continental service, were thus stationed to defend the frontiers of New York, not half so much exposed as Vermont, and, to add to the distress, New York re-called, at the same time, all her state troops from Skeenesborough; in either case, the enemy must come up Lake Champlain, and it would be impossible, then, to reach Fort George without light boats, which they must bring with them, and then they would be obliged to carry them over a 159 neck of land, two miles and a half in length, which connected the two lakes (Champlain and George) where neither cattle nor horses could be found to assist them, and if they even should conquer these difficulties, and lose their boats by any accident, a defeat would be fatal; for it would be almost impossible to secure a retreat, as the mountains on both sides Lake George were extremely difficult to pass; when the enemy might come into Lake Champlain, within twelve miles of Castleton, or, in one day's march through a pleasant country, from opposite to Ticondaroga to Pitsford or Castleton, at each of which places the troops of Vermont were stationed, and, to the south of them, the inhabitants of termont remained on their farms. [The reader is referred to the Map of Vermont and said lakes, annexed to this book, for a more clear idea of these facts.]

Thus Vermont was left to take care of itself, when a frontier to those claiming States, viz. New Hampshire, Massachusett's, and New York, and they using every method to divide its citizens. Congress had also interfered with the internal politics of Vermont, in favour of the claiming States, to cut off her ways and means of raising men and money for self-defence, as will appear from the following resolution of Congress, viz. "Resolved unanimously, That in the opinion of Congress, no unappropriated lands or estates, which are or may be adjudged forfeited, or confiscated, lying in

160 in said district, ought, until the final decision of Congress in the premises, be granted or sold."

The inhabitants of Vermont had rendered themselves obnoxious to the British by the capture of Forts Ticondaroga, Crown Point, and St. John's, the battle of Bennington, cutting off the left wing of General Burgeyne's army, &c. and in Canada there were more British troops than the whole militia and troops in Vermont amounted to altogether.

Thus left, as she had reason to suppose, by the intrigues of those who claimed and coveted her fertile soil, to be a prey to the common enemy, similar to the fate of their brethren, descendants from Connecticut, settled at Wyoming and Susquehannah, who were mostly killed by Colonel Butler and a party of Indians; their towns, villages, &c. burnt, and their country depopulated (supposed to be through the intrigues of the Pennsylvania land-jobbers) which has since become a prey to the Pennsylvania claimants, a junto similar to the New York monopolists, who were then taking every measure that the malignancy and avarice of human nature could suggest, for the destruction of the people of Vermont. But her sons were not to be dismayed by dangers, or depressed in adversity; that in such a crisis their breasts glowed with the real fire of patriotism. The genius of Vermont was fruitful in resources; even in the gulph of difficulties, and on the verge of 161 ruin, she waxed strong, extended her wings, and made herself known amongst the nations of the earth.

In April, 1781, Colonel Ira Allen was appointed by the Governor and Council to settle a cartel with the British in Canada for an exchange of prisoners, and also to procure an armistice between Vermont and the British, which most of the Cabinet Council thought impracticable, at least, for any length of time, as the British had 10,000 troops in Canada, who would in that case, be idle, not being able to annoy the other States without first annoying Vermont. An armistice was necessary for Vermont, as their whole militia did not exceed 7000 men able to bear arms, (her unions excepted) and who could not contend with 10,000 British troops, be maintained and paid, for any length of time, if called out to action; therefore an armistice must be obtained, or the frontiers must be evacuated, until assistance could come from those very States whose influence had rendered Vermont defenceless, which, perhaps, had been contemplated, that they might more easily divide the spoil under a ratification of Congress, and have their troops ready to guarantee such division.

The

The business was necessarily of a private nature; nothing could be written with safety to Vermont; one person was better than more, as cross questions might arise, and no one could divine what questions and propositions might come from the British, respecting the past and future conduct and intentions of the principal characters of Vermont. Besides, there was much danger in the negociation to the Governor, Council, and especially their agent, from the spies of the claiming States and Congress, who would labour hard for proof of a criminal correspondence, to expose life and property; but it was considered, that unless this measure was pursued, there was danger of being annihilated as a State, and being subjected by a power greatly promoted by the exertions of the people of Vermont. Under these circumstances, perseverance in an attempt to obtain an armistice was resolved on, at every possible hazard. At this time only eight persons were in the secret, but more were added as circumstances required. Colonel Allen preferred the first day of May (it being the anniversary of his birth) for his departure on this important business; he took with him one subaltern*, two serjeants, and sixteen privates, and, with a fair wind, soon arrived at *l'Isle aux Noix*, and was kindly and politely received by Major Dundas, Commandant at that place, who provided convenient apartments for Colonel Allen and his suite, and he daily dined with him at the mess. The next day the commissioners met to settle a cartel for the exchange of prisoners; Major Dundas, Captain Sherwood, and George Smyth, Esq; produced their credentials, as also Colonel Allen, and they adjourned to the following day. Captain Sherwood walking next morning with Colonel Allen, told him that Major Dundas had no knowledge of any business, except the exchange of prisoners, and that he and Mr. Smyth were the commissioners to settle the armistice, and to concert with him measures to establish Vermont a colony under the crown of Great Britain. Whether Major Dundas was or not unacquainted with the main business, he conducted himself as if he was not, for which reason the papers respecting the exchange of prisoners were kept by themselves for public inspection. What concerned the armistice was more verbal than written. In the conferences respecting the temper and disposition of the inhabitants of Vermont, and their extreme hatred to the system and government of New York, it was observed, that Congress was making use of every art to bring Vermont in subjection to New York, and that the people of Vermont would, rather than yield to it, see Congress subjected to the British government, provided Vermont could be a distinct colony

* Lieutenant Simeon Lyman.

under

under the crown on safe and honourable terms; that the people
of Vermont were not disposed any longer to assist in establishing a
government in America which might subject them and their posterity to New York, whose government was more detested than
any in the known world, and under which the people of Vermont
164 could never be safe, in person or property, therefore they
would not submit to be subjected to the jurisdiction of New
York on any terms; that the most discerning part of the citizens
were weary of the war, and turning their attention to retirement
and safety, but how to effect their objects was the question.

The replication to the foregoing observations was, that the territory of Vermont could be a colony under the Crown, with privileges equal to those enjoyed by any other colony, and that those
who assisted in effecting such an event, would be duly honoured
and rewarded.   Both parties joined in opinion, that Vermont must
become a British colony, but the methods to effect it, consistent
with the interests of both, were to be discovered.   Much conversation passed on the subject, and Captain Sherwood wrote to General Haldimand, and stated matters, but nothing was decisively
done for some time.   The negociations caused the army to remain
inactive, which gave Colonel Allen reason to persevere with hopes.

Colonel Allen asked leave to go and wait on General Haldimand at Quebec, but was refused; when he wrote General Haldimand, in abstruse terms, on the subject of his mission.   General
Haldimand answered his letter, and sent Major Lunno, Adjutant
General of the army, to join the Commissioners at Isle aux Noix.
165 On his arrival, he had a long conference with the two other
Commissioners, after which a private interview took place between the parties in a bye part of the island, unknown to Major
Dundas, respecting the armistice, and the motives which induced
the people of Vermont to consent to become a British colony.   The
next day Colonel Allen and Major Lunno met at the same place,
and the Major requested Colonel Allen to put down in writing the
most important matters for the consideration of the Commander in
Chief, who would then come to a final conclusion.   Colonel Allen
declined writing any thing on the subject, lest his writings should
be exposed (which would be dangerous to him in the States, and
destroy his influence there) as he had wrote to General Haldiman, and, by accident, the copy of his letter, which was couched
in very ambiguous terms, was enclosed to Major Dundas, who was
angry to think Colonel Allen had wrote off the island without his
consent, and declared to the officers that he would confine Colonel
Allen in irons; the impropriety of which was urged by the officers,
as

as there could be and was no harm in it, as it was to the Commander in Chief, who had duly answered it. Colonel Allen said, he
would verbally state the business, which Major Lunno might write
and communicate to the Commander in Chief with perfect safety
and secrecy, on which the whole business depended, as the zealous
Whigs would listen to no proposals until they saw and felt the
benefits of an armistice; and the loyal subjects, who were scat-
166 tered through the State, must be employed to change the
minds of the Whigs by degrees. Major Lunno at once
adopted Colonel Allen's mode to inform the Commander in Chief,
and proceeded in the following manner :——

Question.—Did not the people of Vermont take an early and
active part in the rebellion ?

Answer.—The people of Vermont were informed that hostilities
had commenced at Lexington, by an express from the Governor
and Council of Connecticut to Colonel Ethan Allen, who requested
him immediately to raise the Green Mountain Boys, and, without
loss of time, to march and take the forts Tycondaroga and Crown
Point, which Colonel Allen complied with, and also took the
King's sloop of war with 16 guns, then lying off Fort St. John's.[1]

Question.—Have the people of Vermont continued their exertions in the course of the war ?

Answer.—No people in America have exerted themselves more
than those of Vermont; they, with the assistance of the militia
from the State of New Hampshire, and from the county of Berkshire, gave the first check to General Burgoyne's army by the victory at Bennington, and by other exertions, greatly contributed to
the capture of his whole army at Saratoga.

167 *Question.*—What were the motives which stimulated the
people of Vermont to such violent measures ?

Answer.—The inhabitants of Vermont principally came from
Connecticut and the other New England States, and, as brethren,
felt for them in a high degree when hostilities first commenced;
besides, they were of the same opinion as entertained by their
brethren in New England, that the Parliament of Great Britain

---

[1] [Benedict Arnold was in the immediate command of the party that
captured the king's sloop.]

had

had no right to bind and control the colonies in all cases whatsoever, and that representation ought to precede taxation.

Question.—On what principles do the people of Vermont act by
endeavouring to obtain an armistice, and the privilege of being a
colony under the crown, after taking so decided a part as you say,
on similar principles to those of their brethren in New England?

Answer.—When the people of Vermont first took an active part
against Great Britain: they were in principles agreed with their
brethren in the other colonies to oppose the claims of the Parliament on America, and fought in their country's cause, expecting to
enjoy equal privileges with their neighbours in chusing and establishing their own form of government, and in sharing with them
all the advantages which might result from their united efforts in
the common cause. But after all, they have found to their
168 sorrow, by acts and resolutions of Congress, and proceedings
of other States, that they intend to annihilate the new State of
Vermont, and annex its territory to New York, whose goverment
is perfectly hated and detested by the people of Vermont. To effect this plan, the frontiers of Vermont have been left naked and
exposed to the wasting sword of the British troops, with a view to
depopulate the country, and give the New York monopolists possession. This usage being too much for human nature to bear,
the citizens of Vermont think themselves justifiable, before God
and man, in seeking an armistice with the British, and ceasing
further to support a power that has too soon attempted to inslave
a brave and generous people.

Question.—Should the Commander in Chief consent to an armistice with Vermont for the time being, and admit it to be a British colony, with as extensive privileges as any colony ever had,
what would be an adequate compensation for the inactivity of the
army? and how soon can Vermont furnish a regiment to be put
on the establishment, and march with the army against Albany,
and what other assistance can Vermont give in such an expedition?

Answer.—The advantages to Great Britiain by making an armistice, and receiving Vermont as a colony, will be great. After
169 the propositions of Colonel Beverly Robinson, in his letter of
March 30, 1780, to General Ethan Allen, the Cabinet Council
of Vermont have not been inattentive to a peace and union with
the British government. Governor Chittenden last July sent a
flag to the British Commodore on Lake Champlain, with a letter to
General Haldimand, requesting the exchange of some prisoners,
                                                              which

which produced a truce last autumn. General Ethan Allen included the frontiers of New York to Hudson's River with Vermont, which produced very good effects, and made the people,
among whom are many loyalists, on that district, friendly and
anxious to come under the jurisdiction of Vermont. The Legislature of Vermont, on their petition, and in consequence of measures
New York, &c., were pursuing against her, extended her jurisdictional claim over that part of New York ; the territory thus added to the State of Vermont is bounded south by a line due west
from the south-west corner of Vermont to the Hudson's River,
thence up the said river to its source, and by a line due north·to
the south line of Canada, thence east to the north-east corner of
Vermont. Articles of union are forming, and no doubt but that
district will be duly represented in the next session of the Legislature of Vermont. In like manner has been added to the jurisdiction of the State, on petition of the inhabitants, all the territory
lying east of Connecticut River, and west of Mason's patent, which
takes away, at least, one-third part of the State of New Hamp-
170 shire. These additional territories will give strength to Vermont and weaken Congress. The extent of country and the
return of such a body of people to their allegiance, with the effects it may have on the people in the other States, many of whom
are sick of the dispute, in consequence of the taxes and hardships
already experienced, most likely will be of greater consequence
than the operation of an army of ten thousand men. As to an
army marching against Albany, it will operate against the union
of the New York district, and that of New Hampshire, now forming with Vermont. This business requires time and moderation,
with the address of some discreet loyalists now in Canada, who
may visit their friends in those districts, and let them know that
Vermont is on good terms with the British.

In Vermont are plenty of men who would be fond of commissions on the British establishment, and could raise a regiment in a
few weeks; but this, with sundry other things, can be better as-
certained after the session of the general Assembly, at Bennington, next June.

A cartel for an exchange of prisoners was compleated. Thus
terminated this negociation in May, 1781, after seventeen days,
on a verbal agreement, that hostilities should cease between the
British and those under the jurisdiction of Vermont, until after the
session of the Legislature of Vermont, and until a reasonable
time after, for a commissary of prisoners to come on board the
Royal

171 Royal George in Lake Champlain, and even longer, if prospects were satisfactory to the Commander in Chief.

In the mean time Vermont was to consolidate her unions to weaken Congress, permit letters to pass through Vermont, to and from Canada, and take prudent measures to prepare the people for a change of Government.

The Commissioners parted in high friendship, and Major Dundas furnished Colonel Allen and his suite with ample stores to return home. On Colonel Allen's return to Castletown, Captain Hurlbert and others waited on him, and desired to be advised whether to remain or move to the interior parts of the country; the Colonel advised them to remain quiet on their farms; that the Governor and Council would provide the best means for their safety; that they must not be surprised if there was not a powerful army to protect the frontiers; should any event make it necessary, for the safety of their families, to move, they might depend on seasonable information: he had a similar interview with Major Hebar Allen, the Rev. Mr. Hibbard, &c. in Poultney.

The Colonel went to Sunderland, and made his report to the Governor and Council, who took measures to carry into effect the stipulations he had made. In June, the Assembly met at Bennington, and received the Representatives from the east and west unions.

172 Many jealousies having arose amongst the zealous whigs in the United States and Vermont, that some negociations were carrying on between the British in Canada and Vermont, which occasioned several men of discernment to be sent from the neighbouring States, as well as many in Vermont, to collect and see, if, at the sessions of the Legislature, they could find any measures were pursuing that might eventually be injurious to the United States, or the common cause of America.

On the other hand, the British in Canada were anxious to know whether Colonel Allen and his friends would be faithful, and conduct matters so as to give a reasonable prospect of success, that might be adequate to a further suspension of hostilities; with these views, two opposite parties attended the Legislature; as the Assembly convened in the Meeting-House, the spectators sat in the galleries.

In

In a few days after their meeting, the Assembly sent a message to the Governor and Council, requesting them to join in committee of both Houses on the subject of Colonel Allen's mission to the British in Canada, &c. The Governor and Council attended in the Assembly, and resolved both Houses into a Committee of the whole, when the Governor proceeded to state the facts ; that in consequence of application from several persons, praying that some measures might be taken to procure the exchange of their 173 friends, who were prisoners in Canada, in the recess of the Legislature, he had, with the advice of Council, appointed and authorized Colonel Ira Allen to go to Isle-aux-Noix to settle a cartel for the exchange of prisoners, in behalf of the State. That Colonel Allen went to the Isle-aux-Noix, where he met the British Commissioners, and with difficulty had compleated the business, in behalf of Vermont, though no such exchange had taken place with the United States, or any other State in the northern department ; that if the grand Committee wished for further particulars, respecting the mission and conduct of Colonel Allen, he was then present and could best inform, to whom he referred them.

The Committee then requested Colonel Allen to inform them respecting his commission, and what effects it had produced. Colonel Allen rose, and observed to the Committee, that he had received an appointment and commission from the Governor and Council, to go and settle a cartel with the British, in Canada, for an exchange of prisoners ; that he had very happily succeeded in his mission, and made his report to the Governor and Council ; but not expecting to be called on by the Committee, had left the commission and all the papers at home ; nevertheless, was ready to give a verbal statement of the whole transactions, or, if more agreeable to the Committee, he would, by leave of the Governor and Council, go home, and produce the writings for the inspection of the Commit- 174 tee next day. The Committee desired Colonel Allen would lay the papers before them the next day.

Accordingly he attended the Committee with the papers, and made a short verbal statement, that the papers might be the better understood ; they were read, and on the whole it appeared, that the British had shewn great generosity in the business. Colonel Allen then rose and stated sundry things, which occurred while he was in Canada, and mentioned that he had discovered among the British officers a fervent wish for peace ; and that the English Government was as tired of the war, as the United States ; then concluded with a desire, that if any Member of the Committee
tee

tee or auditor in the gallery, wished to ask any further questions respecting the business, he was ready to answer them.

All seemed satisfied that nothing had been done inconsistent to the interest of the States ; and those who were in the interest of the United States paid their compliments to Colonel Allen, for his open and candid conduct. In the evening he had a conference with the Canadian spectators on the business of the day, and they appeared to be as well satisfied as those from the neighboring States and Vermont. Is it not curious to see opposite parties perfectly satisfied with one statement, and each believing what they wished to believe, and thereby deceiving themselves ! Major 175 Joseph Fay was then appointed Commissary of prisoners, and after the session of the Assembly, went in July on board the Royal George in Lake Champlain, obtained the exchange of prisoners, and a further extension of the armistice.

In July 1781, General Ethan Allen was informed by one of his neighbors, that some of his friends from Canada wished to speak with him in the dusk of the evening of that day ; that he would shew him the place if he chose to see them ; at the time appointed, General Allen, with his cane only in his hand, cheerfully went to a British guard under arms, and received a packet from the British in Canada. In the twilight of the next day he met them again, and returned an answer ; this mode of correspondence was continued, and whenever dispatches came in this way, General Ethan Allen or Colonel Ira Allen (as they both lived in one house) went and received them and returned an answer, not trusting any other person with these dispatches. It is worthy of remark, that Sunderland, where they lived, was more than sixty miles from the frontiers ; yet a serjeant and six or eight men frequently passed with their arms, in 1781 and 1782, without being discovered by any that would inform against them.

In these times party spirit ran so high against tories, or any correspondence with the British, that a person in Arlington, who 176 had, on these occasions, rendered himself obnoxious to some brave and spirited people in Manchester, &c. a party collected and set out to pull his house down ; their plan was discovered by Colonel Gideon Brownson and Captain Eli Brownson, who met said party in Sunderland, interposed by their advice, to prevent so rash a procedure. Colonel Ira Allen soon came to their assistance ; by their united influence, with difficulty they persuaded said party quietly to return home. That the same evening, Colonel Ira Allen crossing the same ground, where said
party

party were persuaded to return back, met a British guard under arms, received a packet, and returned an answer next evening.

This shews the vicissitudes of human affairs, and the dangers individuals are frequently exposed to, for the best good of the whole.

The Assembly, during their June session, appointed Jonas Fay, Ira Allen, and Bezaleel Woodward, Esquires, agents to Congress. On their way to Philadelphia, and on the same day of their arrival, they, at an inn, saw in a newspaper, a letter from Lord George Germain to Sir Henry Clinton, dated Whitehall, February 7th, 1781, which had been taken by the French and carried to Paris, and by Dr. Franklin forwarded to Congress, who had ordered it to be printed, containing, among other things, the following : " The return of the people of Vermont to their allegiance is an event of the utmost importance to the King's affairs ; and at 177 this time, if the French and Washington really meditate an irruption into Canada, may be considered as opposing an insurmountable bar to the attempt. General Haldimand, who has the same instructions with you to draw over those people, and give them support, will, I doubt not, push up a body of troops, to act in conjunction with them, to secure all the avenues through their country into Canada ; and when the season admits, take possession of the upper parts of the Hudson's and Connecticut rivers, and cut off the communication between Albany and the Mohawk's country. How far they may be able to extend themselves southward or eastward must depend on their numbers, and the disposition of the inhabitants."

This information had greater influence on the wisdom and virtue of Congress, than all the exertions of Vermont in taking Ticondaroga, Crown Point, and the two divisions from General Burgoyne's army, or their petition to be admitted as a State in the general confederation, and offers to pay their proportion of the expenses of the war ; the following resolution will demonstrate it :

" By the United States in Congress assembled, August 7, 1781 : Whereas, the States of New Hampshire and New York have submitted to Congress the decision of the disputes between them, and the people inhabiting the New Hampshire grants, on the west side 178 of Connecticut river, called the State of Vermont, concerning their respective claims of jurisdiction over the said territory, and have been heard thereon ; and whereas the people aforesaid claim and exercise the powers of a sovereign independent

dent State, and have requested to be admitted into the federal
union of the United States in America ; in order thereto, and that
they may have an opportunity to be heard in vindication of their
said claim, Resolved, That a Committee of five be appointed to
confer with such person or persons as may be appointed by the
people residing on the New Hampshire Grants, on the west side
of Connecticut river, or by their representative body, respecting
their claim to be an independent State ; and on what terms it may
be proper to admit them into the federal union of these States, in
case the United States in Congress assembled shall determine to
recognize their independence, and thereon to make report. And
it is hereby further recommended to the people of the territory
aforesaid, or their representative body, to appoint an agent or
agents to repair immediately to Philadelphia, with full powers and
instructions to confer with the said Committee on the matters aforesaid, and on behalf of the said people, to agree upon, and ratify
terms and articles of union and confederation with the United
States of America, in case they shall be admitted into the union.
And the said Committee are hereby instructed to give notice to the
Agents of the States of New Hampshire and New York, to be
present at the conference aforesaid."

179 The said agents arrived in Philadelphia ; saw the preceding resolve of Congress, announced their arrival and mission
to Congress, who appointed a Committee of one member from each
State ; the Committee and Agents had several interviews, in the
course of which the Committee, amongst other things, were in-
quisitive to learn what overtures had been made by the British to
Vermont. On the 18th of August, the following questions and
answers passed in writing between them, viz.

Question 1st. Are the boundaries set forth in the written propositions delivered in by the said Agents at this time, claimed by
the State of Vermont as the lines of jurisdiction, the same as contained in the resolution of Congress of the 7th of August instant ?

Answer. They are the same, with the addition of part of the
waters of Lake Champlain, for the benefit of trade.

Q. 2d. What part do the people of Vermont mean to take as
to the past expences of the present war, and what aid do they
propose to afford as to men and money to the common defence ?

A. Such proportion as shall be mutually judged equitable after
their admission to a seat in Congress, which has been at
                                                    several

several different times officially proposed by Agents on the part of Vermont.

180   *Q. 3d.* What are the ideas of the people of Vermont relative to the claim of private property, under grants or patents from New Hampshire, or New York, previous to the present revolution ?

A. Although the State of Vermont have not hitherto authorized any Courts to take cognizance of such causes as respect titles of lands, nevertheless they have had, and still have it in contemplation to adopt such modes as the circumstances arising out of each case may justify, without adhering to the strict rules of law.

Q. 4th. What are the intentions of your constituents in regard to the patents that were granted on conditions of settlement within a given time, and which have been prevented by the claims of the people of Vermont, and the present revolution ?

A. No forfeitures have been taken by the State of Vermont on any such grants for non-performance of conditions of settlement, and we conceive it to be the intention of our constituents to grant a further reasonable time for fulfilling such conditions.

Q. 5th. What are the number of inhabitants within the lines mentioned in the propositions above mentioned ?

181   *A.* As the citizens of Vermont have not been lately numbered, we can therefore only estimate them at thirty thousand, which we conceive to be nearly a true estimate.

Q. 6th. What quantity of lands is contained within the said bounds ?

A. There has been no accurate survey of the State of Vermont, but we conceive it to contain about five millions of acres.

Q. 7th. What applications have been made, either publicly or privately, by the enemies of the United States, or their adherents, to draw off the people of Vermont from their affection to the United States of America ?

A. The honourable Committee are possessed of copies of Bev. Robinson's letters, inclosed in Brigadier General Allen's letter
of

of 9th of March last, to the then President of Congress, and any private offers we cannot avouch for.

Q. 8th. In case the enemy should attempt an invasion of the northern frontiers, what aid as to men and provisions could be raised in the State of Vermont for the public defence, (you can suppose the invasion made in different quarters) and in what time?

182 *A.* The number of militia within the lines herein limited, we suppose to be about seven thousand, are in general well armed and accoutred, and have ever shown themselves spirited in case of alarms, &c. In regard to provisions, the country is fertile, but new, and considerable emigrations from other States to Vermont.—The Legislature, at their session in October last, levied a tax on the inhabitants sufficient for victualling one thousand five hundred troops in the field for twelve months, and we are of opinion a larger store may be in the same manner collected the ensuing autumn.

Congress then proposed to admit Vermont to be a State, and to have a seat in the union, provided they would relinquish their jurisdiction over lands out of lines to be agreed on and approved in Congress. A Committee of Congress was appointed to meet and agree with the Agents of Vermont, respecting lines and boundaries; they accordingly met. The eastern boundary line proposed by the Committee of Congress was not disputed, but the western boundary afforded a tedious dispute. Mr. James Duane, and Colonel Allen, managed the controversy, both being greatly interested in the lands liable to be affected by the boundary line. Different proposals had been made, without producing any effect, and the Committee often adjourned for deliberation, and went out of the Committee-room in Congress. At length Colonel Allen drew 183 an abstruse line that would answer Vermont; gave it to the late Roger Shearman, Esq. member for Connecticut, just as Congress were impatient to adjourn, praying him to redraft it, and propose it as his own, which he complied with, and laid it before Congress, which was immediately received and passed into a resolve, and Congress adjourned, before Mr. Duane properly understood the motion, or rather, the operation of such proposed line, which added to Vermont beyond the original claim of New Hampshire, (which was a line from the north-west corner of the Massachusett's north, ten degreee east, in the west line of the towns of Pownal, Bennington, Shaftsbury, &c.) the towns of Fairhaven, Benson, South Hero, North Hero, and isle of Mott, and several other Islands, and put out of dispute Alburg, and some other

lands

lands, as also the navigation of Lake Champlain. Had the Legislature of Vermont described Powlet River, instead of Poultney River, in their act of relinquishment of jurisdiction, they would have held a much larger tract, and been equally consistent with the resolve of Congress, and if disputes arose respecting said line, they could not have been used against Vermont, as her Agents did not consent to them.

"August 20, 1781.—Resolved, That it be an indispensable preliminary to the recognition of the independence of the people, inhabiting the territory called Vermont, and their admission into the federal union, that they explicitly relinquish all demands of 184 lands, or jurisdiction, on the east side of the west bank of Connecticut River, and on the west side of a line beginning at the north-west corner of the State of Massachusett's thence running twenty miles east of Hudson's River, so far as said river runs north-easterly in its general course, then by the west bounds of the townships granted by the late Government of New Hampshire, to the river running from South Bay to Lake Champlain, thence along the said river to Lake Champlain, thence along the waters of Lake Champlain to the latitude forty-five degrees north, excepting a neck of land, between Missisqui Bay, and the waters of Lake Champlain.*"

During the time the Agents of Vermont were at Philadelphia, they procured the copy of a letter from the Governor of New Hampshire to the President of Congress, informing that body, that the State could not furnish its quota of men, or money, in support of the war, as a third part of the State had revolted and joined with Vermont, and more towns were expected to follow that example.

In September following, Colonel Allen and Major Fay met the British Commissioners at Skeensborough, to exchange prisoners, when they gave them the copy of the questions and answers of the 185 Committee of Congress and Agents of Vermont on the 18th of August, and also a copy of the letter of the Governor of New Hampshire to the President of Congress.

The Commissioners from Canada were well pleased, and laughed heartily with the Agents from Vermont, who had double the reason to be pleased.

* Journal of Congress, August 20th, 1781, p. 170.

The

The plan of Government for the colony of Vermont was taken into consideration, which was for some time debated, when it was agreed that his Majesty in Council should appoint the Governor, but it was expected to be a subject in the colony; that the people should appoint a Lieutenant Governor and twelve counsellors, who should form one branch of the Legislature, and the other should consist of one member from each town, who were to be annually elected by the people, similar to the present form, who should have a right to enact provincial laws, &c. similar to the colony of Connecticut.

The British Commissioners suggested an instruction from the Commander in Chief, to send scouts and make prisoners of several persons in Vermont, that were most violently opposed to negocia-tions with the British Government.

This, the Agents of Vermont opposed, reprimanding the con-duct of the officer, who presumed to send a scout to and wound 186 Major Younglove, within Vermont, as being a violation of the armistice agreed on ; that every measure of that kind would stimulate a spirit that must be conciliated before a comple-tion of the object wished for.

The object was then relinquished by the Commissioners, as be-ing discretionary with them after a conference with the Agents of Vermont.

The British Commissioners insisted that Vermont should declare itself a British colony, offering to put on the British establish-ment one Brigadier General, two Colonels, and other officers, for two regiments, all to be named by certain men in Vermont, with other advantageous and lucrative offers, proposing an expedition against Albany ; that by uniting the British troops and the Ver-montese, they would form a strong barrier, and be able to defend themselves against the States ; that the Commander in Chief was determined not to lose the campaign inactively ; that something effectual must be determined on before they parted, or the ar-mistice must cease.

The Agents of Vermont treated this proposition with candour and deliberation, stating the local situation of Vermont, and the extent of frontier opposed to the United States to be about two hundred and fifty miles, including her unions bounding on as thick settlements as any in the United States ; that amongst the body of the

187 the people were as staunch whigs as any part of America; that the ties of consanguinity, neighbourly and personal friendship, &c. were opposed to fighting each other; that in the ancient district, as also the unions of Vermont, were some of the most zealous supporters of the independence of America; that to change the temper and disposition of such men, heated with a revolutionary frenzy, must be a work of time and moderation; in the time of an armistice, shewing them the blessings of repose under a permanent Government.

That considering the extent of the frontiers of Vermont, that a range of green mountains divides it near the centre, through which roads were almost impossible; under these considerations, it might not be in the power of his Majesty's troops to defend the said frontiers, especially in the winter, and should they be compelled to retire to Canada, for winter quarters, it would ruin their friends in Vermont, and spoil their best services. The question therefore was, whether, considering the said letter from President Weare to Congress, in which he acknowledges that the State of New Hampshire cannot furnish her quota of men and money for the service of the United States, in consequence of one third part of the State having revolted and joined the new State, and more he expected would follow their example; that another union, to include Berkshire county, in the Massachusett's, might in the 183 course of events take place; that such measures, with their effects on the people through the States, might be of more service to the King's cause than any other thing in the power of Vermont to accomplish.

The British Commissioners took down in writing the heads of those objections, for the information of the Commander in Chief. They then suggested an instruction, which they said they were not at liberty to deviate from without putting an end to the armistice, which was, that his Excellency General Haldimand should, in pursuance of full powers vested in him by his Majesty and Privy Council, to issue his proclamation, offering to confirm Vermont as a colony under the crown, with the full extent of her claims, confirming the principles of Government as aforesaid, provided the people would return to their allegiance; that an army should come up the lake in October, with said proclamations, during the session of the Legislature, and distribute them, when the Legislature must accept the same, and with the British take measures for their common defence, &c.

The Agents of Vermont were unpleasantly situated on these proposals; they reinforced the preceding arguments, with these
remarks,

remarks, that the season was too far advanced for such important operations, considering the climate, badness of roads, that no fortifications or preparations were made on the frontiers for defence, that one winter would have great effect in changing the minds of the people for a new order of things, &c. and that the Commander in Chief, on full consideration of these matters, might be of a different opinion ; but should he not, they hoped the General who brought forward such proclamations, would learn the temper and disposition of the people before he distributed them ; on these principles they consented to have the proclamations brought up the lake, rather than break the armistice.[1]

189

The Commissioners and Agents then separated, on terms of mutual friendship.

In October, 1781, the Legislature met at Charlestown, in the East Unions, when the Government of New Hampshire sent a Major Reynolds, with two hundred men, as was supposed, to stop the election and session of the Legislature ; the friends of Vermont advised the Major, if he had any instructions from New Hampshire, which were hostile to Vermont and the East Union, that it would be for the sake of humanity adviseable for him to keep them to himself, as his force would not avail : this he prudently did, and the Assembly convened and proceeded to business without opposition.   In the mean time, General St. Leger, at the head of the British army from Canada, ascended the Lake Champlain, and rested at Ticondaroga ; while General Enos had the command of the troops of Vermont on the frontiers, and his head quarters at Castleton ; the General, and a number of officers under him, were fully acquainted with the negociations with the British in Canada, in particular Colonels Fletcher and Walbridge. Notwithstanding, it became necessary to keep up appearances, by sending frequently small scouts to Champlain to observe the movements of the enemy.   One of these scouts fell in with a party of General St. Leger's ; some shots were exchanged ; Serjeant Tupper, who commanded the scout from Vermont, was killed on the spot, and his men retreated : the body was decently buried, and General St. Leger sent all his cloaths, with an open letter, to

190

---

[1] [It seems from the *Haldimand Papers* of Sept. 20 and 30 and Oct. 1, 1781, that the author is not quite correct in relation to the origin of the proposal about the proclamations.   It appears to have been made and urged upon the British Commissioners by the Vermont agents, as the only means left them of prolonging the negotiation, and thereby preventing an immediate invasion of the state.   See *H. Hall's   Vt.*, p. 367–369.]

General

General Enos, informing him of his regret for the fate of the sergeant, and made an apology for his death.   Perhaps this was done
to try the spirit and disposition of the inhabitants, previous to the
publication of the proclamation as conceded to at Skeensborough
the September before.   The dispatch and apparel were publicly
delivered to General Enos, which made considerable noise among
the troops : many of them were not acquainted with the subject of
the negociation and armistice ; and some that were, had no objection to raise difficulties, in hopes of gaining popularity.

General Enos, Colonels Fletcher and Walbridge, wrote letters,
and sent immediately an express to Governor Chittenden at
Charlestown, announcing the arrival at Ticondaroga of the British
army ; wherein they blended public matters and private negociation ; Mr. Hathaway, the messenger, not being in the secret,
191 failed not to proclaim the extraordinary message of General
St. Leger through the streets of Charlestown, till he came to the
Governor, which happened in the recess of the Legislature, and
occasioned crowds of people to follow, to hear the news ; the Governor and others were sitting in a large room, amongst whom
were some persons that were eager to learn the negociations that
were generally supposed to be carried on between the British in
Canada and Vermont, to make an ill use thereof.   The Governor
opened one of the letters ; he thought it prudent to peruse it himself before he allowed it to be publicly read.   These letters were
found to contain both public and private information, which occasioned some change of letters between the Governor, Messrs.
Brownson and Fassett, who were in the secret, and next to the
Governor.   In this confused moment, Major Runnals came in, and
enquired of Colonel Ira Allen what was the reason that General
St. Leger was sorry that Sergeant Tupper was killed ?   Mr. Allen
said that he could not tell.   Mr. Runnals repeated the question ;
and Mr. Allen observed, that good men were sorry when good
men were killed, or met with misfortune, which might be the case
with General St. Leger.   This answer enraged Mr. Runnals ; and
he again loudly enquired what reasons could possibly induce a
British General to be sorry when his enemies were killed, and to
192 send his cloaths to the widow ?   Colonel Allen then requested
Major Runnals to go at the head of his regiment, and demand
the reasons of his sorrow, and not stay there asking impertinent
questions, eating up the country's provisions, doing nothing when
the frontiers were invaded.   Very high words passed between the
Major and Colonel Allen, till Mr. Runnals left the room.   This
manœuvre drew all the attention from said letters ; it was then
proposed that the Board of War should be convened ; and the
                                                    Governor

Governor then summoned the members of the Board of War to appear as soon as possible in his chamber, leaving Mr. Hathaway to detail the news to the populace, the Board of War being all in the secret. New letters were made out from General Enos, Colonels Fletcher and Walbridge's letters, and, for the information and satisfaction of the public, read in council and assembly for the originals, and then returned to the Governor. Those letters contained every thing but the existing negociations which prudence and policy dictated to be separated from the other part of said letters.

In the mean time, Colonel Allen and Major Fay wrote to the British Commissioners, who were with General St. Leger, on the subject of their former negociations, in which they gave a list of the names of the members of the Legislature, with marks, denoting the new members, from which the change appeared great. They suggested the capture of Lord Cornwallis and his army, and 193 added that, whether true or not, it had the same effect upon the people, who soon hoped for better news. In this critical situation, they thought it improper to publish the proposed proclamation, as several changes and circumstances seemed to presage more happy events, that should soon make all right. The packet containing Colonel Allen and Major Fay's letter was delivered at Ticondaroga about ten o'clock in the morning. About an hour after, an express arrived from the southward, which was supposed to contain the news of the capture of Lord Cornwallis and his army; for before evening, the troops, stores, &c. were embarked, and with a fair wind returned to Canada. Thus ended the campaign of 1781, with the accidental loss of only one man, on the extensive frontiers of Vermont, exposed to an army of ten thousand men; yet she did not incur any considerable debt. Such were the happy effects of these negociations.

During the session of the Legislature the resolves of Congress of the 7th and 20th of August, 1781, were laid before them, but that body was composed of men of very different interests, and more widely opposed in politics; these resolves were viewed by the several parties according to their objects, which rendered it difficult to come to any determination. However, the Assembly resolved that they could not comply with the resolves of Congress of the 7th and 20th of August, without destroying the foundation 194 of the universal harmony and agreement that subsisted in the State, and a violation of solemn compact entered into by articles of union and confederation; that they would remain firm in the principles on which the State had first assumed Government, and

and hold the articles of union, which connected each part of the
State with the other, inviolate; that they would not submit the
question of their independence to the arbitrament of any power;
but that they were willing and ready to refer the question of their
jurisdictional boundary with New Hampshire and New York, to
Commissioners mutually chosen; and when they should be admitted into the American union, they would submit any such disputes to Congress.

The Legislature then proceeded to pass an act, appointing
Commissioners with full powers to agree with like Commissioners
from the State of New Hampshire, and these to appoint three or
more Commissioners, who, after hearing all parties, were fully
authorized, on the part of Vermont, to establish a boundary line
between said States.

A similar law was passed respecting a boundary line between
the States of New York and Vermont. A question arose concerning the manner of informing the General Court of New
Hampshire of it. Some urged to have it sent by two agents, to be
195 appointed for the purpose, and for them further to negociate
with the Court of New Hampshire, by stating the difficulties
the Legislature labored under in complying with the resolves of
Congress; that the claims of Vermont were necessary to repel the
claims of New Hampshire; that a line settled by Commissioners,
duly authorized by all parties, as all were represented in the Legislatures of New Hampshire and Vermont, would, in fact, be the
act of all concerned, and where every argument might be publicly
discussed before such Commissioners, in vindication of the rights
of all interested; that a line settled in this manner would be more
agreeable to the people, wherever it might be established, than
any mode that could be devised; that a line established by such
Commissioners would be satisfactory to the respective States and
Congress; that it would have good effects on the pending cause of
all America, by the settlement of boundaries and internal discord.
This mode of reasoning equally applied to the settlement of a
boundary line with New York as New Hampshire, yet a majority
in the Legislature of Vermont decided against any agency in the
business, and the acts were sent to New Hampshire and New York
by private conveyance.

The neglect in not sending one or more agents to the General
Court of New Hampshire at this time, was extreme bad policy in
196 Vermont; had she sent agents to have explained matters as
aforesaid, it would have had the appearance of a more serious

ous desire to settle with New Hampshire, and this was then the more necessary, as there were more than suspicions that Vermont was carrying on some negociations with the Government of Great Britain. Under these circumstances, had discreet agents attended the Court of New Hampshire, there cannot be any reasonable doubt but that the Court would have passed a similar law, and proceeded to a settlement on the principles aforesaid.

Had an agent been sent to New York to effect the same object with that State, there is not the least probability that the Legislature would have complied with such measures, in consequence of their extensive claim to lands in the State of Vermont: Indeed, if the author had been the agent, he would not have pressed a compliance very hard, for he would have considered a refusal on the part of that State advantageous to Vermont. In this case, Vermont would have complied with the spirit of the resolves of Congress, so far as existing circumstances would admit, and New York would have been in fault, for not complying with an offer so fair and reasonable, and which had produced an amicable settlement with New Hampshire and Vermont. The consequence would have undoubtedly been, that Vermont would have retained her west union to the present day, if not extended her claims further west, for a settlement with New Hampshire would have 197 made friendship with the States of Massachusett's, Rhode Island, and Connecticut; that the States of New Jersey, Pennsylvania, Delaware and Maryland, would also, in that case, have been friendly to Vermont. Indeed, the four last-mentioned States, from local circumstances and interest in gaining a share in unlocated lands and confiscated estates, obtained by the united efforts of the United States, and which they held, ought to be appropriated to defray the expence of the war, and not for the emolument of any particular State in whose jurisdiction or claim such property was situate.* It is to be observed, that the States of New Jersey, Delaware, and Maryland, had no vacant lands, and that Pennsylvania was limited and proprietary; that an agent from Vermont had assured the Legislators of these States that the people of Vermont were in opinion with them in regard to unlocated lands and confiscated estates; that the Government of New York had contended with all the neighbouring colonies, then States, to extend her boundaries, and her claims to the west were then considered exorbitant. From these interested motives, and the exertions of the people of Vermont in the common cause of America, those

---

* Unlocated lands and confiscated estates were then in question before Congress.

States

States felt a friendship for Vermont. The same interested motives operated in New Hampshire and Rhode Island respecting vacant lands, &c. The people of Massachusett's, Connecticut, and all the New England or neighbouring States, were deeply interested in the new lands of Vermont, both by grants from New Hampshire and Vermont: Indeed, members of Congress, and men of the first honor and influence in these States, were interested in said lands, especially in the grants of Vermont. The ties of consanguinity, neighbourly and personal friendship, had formed a good understanding, and it may be said, with propriety, that this addition to Vermont on the ancient territorial jurisdiction of New York, would have been a satisfactory retaliation to the old opposers of the claims of New York, not only in Vermont, but in the States of Massachusett's, Connecticut, and New Jersey. Under all these circumstances, with the prospects of peace, Vermont would have had but little to fear from Congress or New York, in consequence of her western territory.

The said resolves of Congress of the 7th and 20th of August were taken up in the Legislature of New York ; on the 15th and 19th of November they passed a number of resolutions, and a solemn protest against the proceedings of Congress. Having stated their claims, and related some of the former proceedings of Congress relative to the controversy, they resolved, " That the Legislature of that State was greatly alarmed at the evident intention of Congress, from *political expedience,* to establish an *arbitrary* boundary, which excluded from that State a great part of its territory ; that it was the sense of the Legislature, that Congress had not any authority, by the articles of confederation, to intermeddle with the former territorial extent of jurisdiction or property, of either of the United States, except in cases of dispute between two or more of the States in the union, nor to admit into the union even any British colony, except Canada, without the consent of nine States, nor any other State whatsoever, nor, above all, to create a new State by dismembering one of the thirteen United States, without their universal consent; that in case of any attempt of Congress to carry into execution their acts of the 7th and 20th of August, the Legislature were bound in duty to their constituents to declare the same an assumption of power, and a manifest infraction of the articles of confederation, and do, therefore, solemnly *protest* against the same ; that a copy of their resolutions be transmitted to Congress, and their delegates expressly directed and required to enter

enter their dissent on every step, which may be taken in and towards carrying the said acts of Congress into execution."*

In the preceding resolves of the Legislature of New York are these words, viz. " from *political [expedience* to establish an arbitrary boundary." By this it appears to have been the sense of that Legislature, that the resolves of Congress were the illegitimate offspring of Lord George Germain's orders, dated Whitehall, February 7, 1781, and directed to Sir Henry Clinton, at New York.

In December new scenes of difficulty and danger presented themselves, and the affairs of Vermont appeared fast approaching to an alarming crisis, assailed as she was, at the same time, and threatened by an armed force from New York and New Hampshire.

General Gansevoort, in pursuance of a law of the State of New York, and conformable to the orders of Governor Clinton, was detached with a part of his brigade of militia to assist the Sheriff of the county of Albany to suppress an insurrection in said county, alias the west union of Vermont; Colonel Abbot collected the militia in the union to oppose him; they encamped against each other, and remained in this situation for some time; the horrors of civil war seemed to moderate both parties.

In the mean time Governor Chittenden tried to reconcile both parties by writing, and he also appointed General Safford and Colonel Walbridge to repair there, and, if possible, to settle the controversy in some way, and by all means prevent the shedding of blood. They repaired to the contending parties, and were the means of keeping them more quiet, but could not effect any accommodation.

The Governor then directed Colonel Allen to see if he could devise any means to accommodate matters; for, said the Governor, a civil war is much to be dreaded. Colonel Allen repaired to Colonel Abbot's camp, held a conference with him and his officers, admonishing them against any rash measures; that some way would be found to settle the dispute without an appeal to arms, engaging them not to commence hostilities till the further order of the Governor. He then proceeded to General Gansevoort's camp, had an interview with him and his officers, endeavoured to settle the controversy, observing, that the measures

* Journal of Congress, April 4, 1782, p. 329, 334.

pursued

pursued by New York had necessitated Vermont to extend her claims, that in time of peace the dispute might be adjusted, &c.

General Gansevoort was very much opposed to a civil war, yet thought it a duty incumbent on the State of New York to protect her inhabitants, who owed and professed allegiance to that Government. Colonel Allen observed, that the State of Vermont had an equal right to protect those who had acknowledged her jurisdiction, which was a great majority of the people; that it would be adviseable to use lenient measures on both sides, till a boundary line could be settled by Congress between the States, thereby to 202 prevent the horrors of a civil war, when the united efforts of all were necessary in the common cause against Great Britain; but no measures could be suggested to induce General Gansevoort to withdraw from said union.

Colonel Allen returned to the Governor and Council, advised that the Governor, as Captain General, should direct a sufficient military force to march, from within the old bounds of Vermont against General Gansevoort, as the only means to restore tranquillity without bloodshed; for in that case General Gansevoort would, in his opinion, retreat, and not otherwise. The plan was adopted; and while the Governor was making out his orders, directing Colonel Ira Allen, with a detachment of militia, to prosecute said plan, an express arrived from William Page, Esq; Sheriff of the county of Washington, announcing the prospects of hostilities in the east union from New Hampshire. This intelligence made a serious impression on the minds of the Governor and Council for a few moments (as it appeared like an agreement between the claiming States to commence hostilities at one and the same time.) When they resumed business, Colonel Walbridge was directed to march with a detachment of militia against General Gansevoort. In his way he received a letter from General Gansevoort.

203 At the same time the troops of New York were in motion to suppress the proceedings of their citizens, who had formed an union with Vermont. On December 18, their Commander, Brigadier General Gansevoort, wrote to the commanding officer of the troops from Vermont, that in pursuance of a law of New York, he had been detached with a part of his brigade to suppress an insurrection of some of the inhabitants of Schaticook and Housac; that he was arrived to aid the Sheriff of the County, to apprehend the insurgents; and was informed that a large body of troops from the grants, were marching in force, with artillery; but before he proceeded any further, he wished to be informed
what

what was the object of their movement into the interior parts of
that State, and by what authority.* Colonel Walbridge, commandant of the troops from Vermont, wrote in answer, that the
object of their movement, was to protect those of the inhabitants,
who, in consequence of the union, professed allegiance to the State
of Vermont; that he wished conciliatory methods might be
adopted, but if those persons who professed to be citizens of Vermont should be imprisoned, and their property destroyed, he was
not to be answerable for the consequences.† General Gansevoort
retreated, and peace was restored.

204 The Governor and Council attended to the said dispatches
from William Page, Esq; and appointed Colonel Ira Allen,
and instructed him to repair to the General Court of New Hampshire, then in session at Exeter, with full powers to concert measures for an amicable adjustment of all disputes with that State.
On the 14th Governor Chittenden issued orders to Lieutenant
Governor Payne (who lived in the east union) to raise the militia
east of the Green Mountains to protect the civil authority and inhabitants against the menacing insults of New Hampshire, and
if attacked, to repel force by force.

Colonel Allen took these orders, and proceeded to Charlestown,
and on conferring with William Page, Esq; found a prospect of
hostilities on the eve of commencement, on the part of New
Hampshire, for the protection of some persons who professed allegiance to that State. Col. Allen immediately made out several
copies of said orders to Governor Payne, ostensibly to encourage
the people in the east union to remain firm to Vermont, but found
means for one copy to fall into the hands of a staunch friend to
New Hampshire, who eagerly seized the prize, and sent it by express night and day to the Governor of New Hampshire. Col.
Allen then proceeded to Exeter. On his way through the State,
he found the people extremely enraged against Vermont, both on
account of her supposed connexions with the British in Canada,
205 and for extending her claims, so much to the injury of that
State, that, in fact, very little stimulus would raise the people
to a civil war, which was his duty and inclination, if possible, to
prevent. These circumstances made him apprehensive it might be
difficult to gain the necessary information. When he arrived, and
being acquainted with the late Major General Fulsom, who was
Commandant of all the militia of that State, and had been friendly

* P. Gansevoort's letter of December 18, 1781.
† E. Walbridge's letter of December 19, 1781.

to

to Vermont, Col. Allen, on his arrival, found means immediately to have a private interview with him, by which he learnt, that two days before the Court had determined to raise a sufficient military force to assist the civil power to carry into effect the laws of the State to Connecticut River; that the day before a copy of Governor Chittenden's orders to Lieutenant Governor Payne had been delivered to Mr. Weare, purporting a determination to repel force by force; this had occasioned a delay in issuing said orders; for if the militia to the west of Connecticut River were to cross and oppose the authority of New Hampshire, it would provoke a civil war. Under these circumstances, what further order the Court would take was yet undetermined. This interview was agreed to be kept a profound secret till all disputes were settled between the contending States.

Col. Allen waited on the President and Council, and delivered his credentials, but the President and Council received him coolly, 206 appeared not inclined to make any stipulations whatever respecting Vermont. Indeed their countenance, &c. seemed to whisper, this is the man that has carried on the negociations with the British in Canada, that produced Lord George Germain's instructions to Sir Henry Clinton, &c. purporting an intention of Vermont's being a British colony; he has before learned our secrets and profited thereby; he is a dangerous man, and we must unite and guard against him. No information could be obtained from any member of the Legislature, notwithstanding Mr. Allen was intimately acquainted with many of them.

While Colonel Allen was thus endeavouring to reconcile matters, General Enos and William Page, Esq; arrived with a letter from Lieutenant Governor Payne to President Weare, inclosing the copy of Governor Chittenden's orders to him, informing Mr. Weare that it was his wish to avoid the horrors of civil war, but before the people who had united with Vermont, and were under her protection, should be subjected by any hostile operation of New Hampshire, they would spiritedly oppose her, and that New Hampshire must be responsible for the consequences.

These gentlemen were authorized to assist Colonel Allen in his laudable endeavours to restore harmony. Mr. Page, who had been active in opposing the laws of New Hampshire, and lived on 207 the east side of Connecticut river, was immediately arrested and confined in gaol, as might have been reasonably expected; thus, spirited measures were pursuing on all sides, while no negociation could be entered into by the united exertion of the Agents

of

of Vermont, nor could they learn what determination the Court
had, or would probably come to : all was a profound secret.

In this situation, Colonel Allen engaged a lady to gain for him
the requisite information, which she effected, and informed him
of the time when the business would finally be discussed and determined in the general Court, by both houses in grand Committee.

When the Court convened on this subject, Colonel Allen went
into the lobby, and began to write a memorial to the Legislature
of New Hampshire. In the mean time he heard the debates, and
that the Court determined on appointing an Agent to take the advice of Congress previous to any hostile measures. Colonel Allen
took his leave of General Enos and Mr. Page ; on his return he
wrote to Lieutenant-Governor Payne and the Members of Council
on the east side of the mountain, requesting them to attend in
Council at Arlington, to hear his report, and take such further
steps as might be thought proper.

When the Council had convened, and heard Colonel Allen's
report, they appointed Jonas Fay, Ira Allen, and Israel Curtis,
Esqrs. agents, to attend Congress, who arrived in Phila-
208 delphia the next day after the Agent from New Hampshire,
in February, 1782.

The Agents of Vermont exhibited their credentials to Congress,
and had repeated interviews with Committees and Members of that
body, who appeared very much dissatisfied with the Legislature of
Vermont, in not complying with their resolves of the 7th and 20th
of August. The Agents of Vermont represented, in justification,
that having been deprived of continental aid, while acts and resolutions of Congress were passed in favour of the claiming and
neighbouring States ; and those States assisted by said acts and
resolves, were taking every measure in their power to divide and
sub-divide her citizens ; that the Legislature of New Hampshire
had, against the will of Vermont, laid a jurisdictional claim,
prefaced with friendship, when subsequent transactions shewed
that the object was to overturn her jurisdiction, and connect the
whole territory of Vermont to New Hampshire, for the members
of her General Court had, by circular letters, convened a Convention for the ostensible purpose of connecting the New Hampshire
Grants on both sides of Connecticut river, into one entire State ;
then, on the 16th day of January, 1781, at Charlestown, where
forty-three towns were represented, procured a vote to unite the
whole

whole to New Hampshire; that this was, in fact, to annihilate the existence of Vermont.

209 In this Convention were twelve Members of the Council and Assembly of New Hampshire; surely Congress could not blame the friends of Vermont, who had been silent spectators of these bare-faced intrigues, in exerting themselves next day, and obtaining a resolution of the Convention to unite that part of New Hampshire, west of the Mason line, to Vermont; this was turning the same trouble on New Hampshire that she had contemplated for Vermont, and was the more justifiable, as it united her citizens, and made her more formidable against her enemies, which was essential, considering the extent of her frontiers. That the claims and intrigues of New York, and self-preservation, had induced the Legislature of Vermont to claim a part of the State of New York; that the people of these territories had, by articles of union, confederated with Vermont, and became citizens thereof; her conduct might be further justified by the articles of union with said districts; in them it was stipulated, that whenever Vermont was acknowledged as a State by Congress, and admitted to a seat in that body, any dispute that might exist respecting boundary lines should be submitted to Congress for decision; that Vermont then was, and ever had been ready and willing to comply with the aforesaid principles, or any other equitable mode that might be agreed upon to settle boundary lines with either of the claiming States; but that she will not, under existing circumstances, dissolve her unions, agreeable to the late resolves of Congress, thereby weakening her strength without gaining an equivalent by a confederation;

210 that if the United States were serious in admitting Vermont into the union, they could not see why it might not be done in the first instance, and then settle the boundary lines on principles that might be equitable and consistent with the articles of the confederacy of the United States, and articles of the unions which necessity had compelled her to make; and further that the Legislature of Vermont, in October last, passed an act, appointing Commissioners, with full powers to agree with like Commissioners from New Hampshire and New York, and they to appoint three or more Commissioners, to hear and determine on boundary lines between the respective States, which line or lines so determined on, should be boundaries between said States, which act was sent to the Legislatures of New Hampshire and New York, with a request that they would respectively pass similar acts, and attend to a settlement of boundary lines. Now had either of these States seriously wished for a settlement of boundary lines, and to admit Vermont into the confederacy, why did they not pass
acts

acts similar to that of Vermont, or, at least, withdraw their jurisdictional claim from the ancient territory of Vermont, instead of
menacing a State with military operations, who, of all others,
were most exposed to the common enemy, and recently deprived of
continental aid.

With respect to a civil war, at a time when the liberty of America
would thereby be endangered, no people were or could be more
averse to it than those of Vermont, who had been eight years
211 longer struggling for their liberties than their brethren of the
United States. As to Governor Chittenden's orders to Lieutenant Governor Payne and Colonel Walbridge, so much complained
of, extraordinary cases required extraordinary remedies, and
these orders, like sovereign balsams, had a salutary effect, as the
consequences evince; for at least they prevented the effusion of
blood and civil war, as they caused General Gansevoort to retreat, when he saw a force was advancing to reinforce those he
was menacing; and the Government of New Hampshire suspended
their military operations on discovering the determination of Vermont, while peace was restored without bloodshed, which otherwise, in all probability, would not have taken place. This also
evinces the sagacity and independence of the Governor; and un-
questionably such a suggestion of facts and cogent arguments had
a very powerful effect upon Congress; for on March 1st it was
proposed in Congress to pass a resolve, that if within one month
from the time in which the resolve should be communicated to
Thomas Chittenden, the inhabitants of Vermont should comply
with the resolves of August 7th and 20th, 1781, they should be
immediately admitted into the union; but if they should refuse
this, and did not desist from attempting to exercise jurisdiction
over the lands guaranteed to New Hampshire and New York,
Congress would consider such neglect or refusal, as a manifest in-
212 dication of designs hostile to the United States, and that all
the pretensions and applications of the said inhabitants, heretofore made for admission into the federal union, were falla-
cious and delusive; and that thereupon the forces of the United
States should be employed against the inhabitants, and Congress
would consider all the lands within the territory to the eastward
of the ridge of mountains as guaranteed to New Hampshire; and
all the lands to the westward of said line, as guaranteed to New
York; and that the Commander in Chief of the armies of the
United States do without delay or further order carry these resolutions into full execution. But after warm debates, and repeated
trials, a vote could not be obtained to adopt these resolutions,
and the matter subsided.

By

By these proceedings, it is easy to discover that they were the vindictive efforts of an almost exhausted political adversary, who found few supporters in Congress. Vermont had then become strong and consequential in her unions, numbers, and unanimity of her citizens.

By her exertions in the common cause of America.

By the liberal offers she had made to Congress to bear her proportion in the expence of men and money in the prosecution of the war.

213   By her equitable offers for the settlement of boundary lines, &c. with the claiming States.

By ties of consanguinity in the neighbouring States.

By the disposal of certain proportions of her fertile soil to many respectable and influential citizens of the United States.

By her *more than supposed* negociation with Great Britain and *northern key*.

With these advantages she held of herself a Congress, or a political balance against Congress and the claiming States, that hostilities could not be commenced against her by them, without endangering the very existence and independence of the United States.

The Agents of Vermont having negociated so far as they supposed necessary for her safety, being fully convinced that no decision under existing circumstances would pass in Congress against her; and feeling an anxiety to learn the proceedings of the Legislature, took their leave of Congress about the 22d of February, 1782, and set out for Bennington with all possible speed. At Colonel Griffing's in the Fish-kills, in the State of New York, they met the unwelcome tidings that the Legislature had dissolved her unions; and proceeding to Bennington, found that the Legislature was adjourned, and the members left town the day 214   before; that the Governor and Council were attending to business at Shaftsbury, to which place they repaired, and found them making out credentials and instructions to the Delegates appointed by the Legislature to negociate the admission of Vermont into the federal union, &c. A question then arose, and the opinion of said Agents was required by the Governor and Council, whether Vermont

mont would, after complying with the resolves of Congress, be admitted into the federal union ? The Agents answered, that in their opinion Vermont would not be admitted ; that she had, by dissolving her union, weakened her strength, lessened her consequence, and exposed herself to the sport of state politicians ; and her safety much depended on the events of peace or war.

Thus while the preceding measures were carrying on in Philadelphia, the Legislature of Vermont, without waiting the advice or arrival of their Agents from Congress, became the dupes of state politicians, precipitately dissolved their unions, lessened their strength, real and political consequence.[1]

The following were the legislative proceedings on that occasion :——

<small>STATE OF VERMONT, IN GENERAL ASSEMBLY,</small>
Feb. 22, 1782.

" The recommendation of the grand Committee, consisting of his Excellency the Governor, the Honourable the Council, and the 215 Representatives of the People, on taking into consideration the resolutions of Congress respecting this State, in the month of August last (being read) is as follows : That in the sense of this Committee, Congress, by their resolutions of August last, in guaranteeing to the States of New York and New Hampshire respectively, all the territory, without certain limits therein expressed, has eventually determined the boundaries of this State.—And whereas it appears to this Committee consistent with the spirit, true intent, and meaning of the articles of union entered into by this State with the inhabitants of a certain district of country on the east side of the west banks of Connecticut river, and on the west side of a line twenty miles east of Hudson's

---

[1] [Although the legislature and people of Vermont were disappointed in their expectations that their compliance with the terms proposed by Congress would secure their speedy admission into the federal union, yet few of their number probably concurred with Mr. Allen in regreting the measure. By it they had retained all the territory they had originally claimed, had averted the danger of civil war with New Hampshire and New York, and having done all that had been required of them by Congress, the justice of their claim to independence could not thereafter be successfully controverted before the world, by either Congress or New York,—the legislature of that State having voluntarily submitted the decision of the controversy to that body.]

river,

river, which articles of union were executed on the 25th day of February, and the 15th day of June last, that Congress should consider and determine the boundary lines of the State : It is recommended to the Legislature of this State to pass resolutions declaring their acquiescence in, and accession to the determination made by Congress of the boundary lines between the States of New Hampshire and New York respectively, and this State, as they are in said resolutions defined and described. And also, expressly relinquishing all claims to, and jurisdiction over, the said districts of territory without said boundary lines, and the inhabitants thereon residing.

216 " Confiding in the faith and wisdom of Congress, that they will immediately enter on measures to carry into effect the other matters in the said resolution contained, and settle the same on equitable terms, whereby this State may be received into, and have and enjoy all the protection, rights, and advantages of a federal union with the United States of America, as a free, independent, and sovereign State, as is held forth to us in and by the said resolutions :

" And that the Legislature cause official information of their resolutions to be immediately transmitted to the Congress of the United States, and to the States of New Hampshire and New York respectively.

" Whereupon resolved,

" That the foregoing recommendation be complied with, and that the west banks of Connecticut river, and a line beginning at the north-west corner of the State of Massachusetts, from thence northward twenty miles east of Hudson's river, as specified in the resolutions of Congress in August last, be considered as the east and west boundaries of this State. That this Assembly do hereby relinquish all claims and demands to, and right of jurisdiction in and over any and every district of territory, without said boundary lines. That authentic copies of this resolution be forthwith officially transmitted to Congress, and to the States of New Hampshire and New York respectively."

217 The Legislature of Vermont having fully complied with the resolves of Congress, proceeded to appoint Agents and Delegates to Congress, and requested the Governor to commission them with plenary powers to negotiate the admission of Vermont into the confederacy of the United States, and to sign articles of

perpetual

perpetual union and confederation ; and when compleated, two of
them were to take their seats and represent Vermont in Congress.

The Agents and Delegates were accordingly commissioned by
the Governor in Council for the purposes aforesaid, and proceeded
to Philadelphia; and on the 31st of March, 1782, exhibited to
Congress their credentials, with the act of the Legislature of
Vermont, dissolving her unions, and fully complying with the resolves of Congress of the 7th and 20th of August, 1781.   These
matters were referred to a Committee of Congress, who reported,
on the 17th of April, 1782, that " In the sense of your Commit-
mittee, the people of the said district, by the last recited act, have
fully complied with the stipulation made and required of them, in
the resolutions of the 7th and 20th of August, as preliminary to
a recognition of their sovereignty and independence, and admission into the federal union of the States.   And that the *condi-
tional* promise and engagement of Congress of such recognition,
and admission, is thereby become *absolute* and *necessary* to be
performed.   Your Committee therefore submit the following reso-
tion :

218   " That the district or territory called Vermont, as defined
and limited in the resolutions of Congress of the 7th and
20th of August, 1781, be, and it is hereby recognized, and acknowledged by the name of the State of Vermont, as free, sovereign, and independent ; and that a Committee be appointed to treat
and confer with the Agents and Delegates from said State, upon the
terms and mode of the admission of the said State into the federal
union."—When this report was read in Congress, a motion was
made and seconded, that the first Tuesday in October next be assigned for the consideration of the report : The vote passed in
the negative.   A motion was then made and seconded, that the
third Tuesday in June next be assigned for the consideration of
the report.   The vote was again in the negative.   A motion was
then made and seconded, that Monday next be assigned for the
consideration of the report ; and the vote was also found in the
negative, for the third time.

From these proceedings of Congress, and other information
which the Agents of Vermont had obtained, they found that Congress had adopted their old policy and procrastination ; they therefore closed their business on the 19th of April, in a letter to the
President of Congress, representing that Vermont, in consequence
of the faith which Congress had pledged to them, had been prevailed upon to comply with their resolutions, in the most ample
manner

manner ; that they were disappointed by the unexpected delay of
219 Congress, in not executing, on their part, the intent and
spirit of the resolve ; that Vermont was now reduced to
a critical situation, by casting off a considerable part of her
strength, in being exposed, as a forlorn hope, to the main force of
the enemy in Canada, and destitute of the aid of the United
States ; which made them urgent that unnecessary delay might not
deprive them of the benefit of the confederation ; and that they
should expect to be officially acquainted when their attendance
would be necessary.

It may not be improper to revert to and trace the principal
causes that induced the Legislature of Vermont to dissolve her
unions, and in the first place to consider the principles upon which
her members justified their conduct in the act of dissolving said
unions. Different considerations induced the Legislature to extend her jurisdictional claims, as have been already stated ; but
the unions consisted of a number of articles between the Legislature of Vermont on the one part, and the Representatives
of the people of the respective districts in Convention on the
other, amongst which were two articles of the following import :
that the Legislature reserved a right to dissolve such union, in
case any event should endanger the existence of the State of Vermont in consequence of such union. That the final arbitrament
and settlement of boundary lines should be submitted to the
final discussion of Congress.

220 The Legislature considered the resolves of Congress of the
7th and 20th of August, as coming within the spirit and
meaning of said articles, that Congress had settled her boundaries, and that a longer refusal to comply with said resolves
might endanger the existence of the State.

The resolve of the 7th of August was delivered to Governor
Chittenden by Ezra Hecock, Esq. with a verbal message from
General Washington, to know whether the people of Vermont
would be satisfied with the independence proposed by Congress,
or whether they had seriously contemplated to join the enemy,
and become a British colony ? By this it appears that the instructions of Lord George Germain to Sir Henry Clinton had awak-
ened the attention of Congress and the General to the cause of
Vermont, and that there was an understanding between them for
the interference of General Washington, as also appeared in the
course of the conference between Messrs. Chittenden and Hecock, who being intimate acquaintances, conversed freely on the
subject ;

subject; in the course of which, Governor Chittenden described
the situation and necessities Vermont had been reduced to by the
claims of the neighbouring States and Congress; the defenceless
State of the frontiers; the power of the British in Canada; that
the people of Vermont had been zealous supporters of the independence of America; but since deserted by them, were at liberty
221 to form such connections as self-preservation might dictate,
and were at liberty to, and desirous of, becoming one of the
United States. Notwithstanding all that had passed between the
agents of Vermont and the British agents in Canada, giving a
short state of these matters, as being necessary for the defence
of the frontiers, &c. Governor Chittenden then requested Mr. Hecock to make a verbal statement thereof to General Washington
on his return.

On further consideration of these matters, and the refusal of
the Legislature in October to comply with the resolves of Congress of the 7th and the 20th of August, Governor Chittenden, on
the 14th of November, wrote a letter to General Washington on
the subject, in unequivocal terms—That there were no people on
the continent more attached to the cause of America than the people of Vermont, but that they were fully determined not to be
put under the government of New York, and would oppose it by
force of arms, and join with the British in Canada, rather than
submit to that government; for they had as good a right to choose
what form of government they would establish for the government
of their internal police, as the United States had to assume and
establish government for themselves, on the principles of the revolution of America.

The danger of a civil war between New York and Vermont,
also between New Hampshire and Vermont, with the effects such
222 measures might have on the pending cause of the United
States, gave great concern to Congress, and the Commander
in Chief was induced to interfere, for the accommodation of a controversy dangerous to the existence of the independence of the
United States. On the first of January, 1782, the General answered Governor Chittenden's letter, in the course of which are
these words, viz.

" It is not my business, neither do I think it necessary now, to
discuss the origin of the right of a number of inhabitants to that
tract of country, formerly distinguished by the name of the New
Hampshire grants, and now known by that of Vermont. I will
take it for granted that their right was good, because Congress,
by

by their resolve of the 7th of August, imply it; and by that of
the 20th, are willing fully to confirm it, provided the new State is
confined to certain described bounds. It appears, therefore, to
me, that the dispute of boundary is the only one that exists, and
that being removed, all other difficulties would be removed also,
and the matter terminated to the satisfaction of all parties. You
have nothing to do but withdraw your jurisdiction to the confines
of your old limits, and obtain an acknowledgement of independence and sovereignty, under the resolve of the 20th of August,
for so much territory as does not interfere with the ancient established bounds of New York, New Hampshire, and Massachusetts.
In my private opinion, while it behooves the delegates to do ample
223 justice to a body of people, sufficiently respectable by their
numbers, and entitled by other claims to be admitted into
that confederation, it becomes them also to attend to the interests
of their constituents, and see, that under the appearance of justice
to one, they do not materially injure the rights of others. I am
apt to think this is the prevailing opinion of Congress."

The universal confidence that the people of America placed in
their Commander in Chief, from the firm, steady, persevering, and
able manner he had conducted the war; his known integrity, wisdom, and virtue gave him more influence over the Legislature of
Vermont than any other man in existence.

The additional population, and consequence of some persons in
the Unions tended to distribute public offices, and affect the popularity of more than one. Some prejudices remained that were im-
bibed by the presiding [preceding] union of sixteen towns, the
Cornish convention of the 9th of December, 1778, &c. Some were
precipitately ambitious to gain seats in Congress. Many wished to
put an end to a controversy that seemed to threaten the utmost
danger, considering these measures consistent with the articles of
union as aforesaid. Placing unlimited confidence in the Commander in Chief, they were induced to rely on the resolves of
Congress, which they had before treated as the effects of the in-
224 trigues of their cruel adversaries, who had caused the frontiers of Vermont to be left defenceless.

On these principles two unions were dissolved, which were
formed through necessity and retaliation; in which Vermont
shewed a superior policy, by drawing in the people to unite under
the government; which, from their formation, had been adding
numbers, strength, popularity, &c.; hence procrastination weakened the resources and strength of Congress; added proportionate
power

power and consequence to Vermont; prevented a division of the
State, and contributed much towards its establishment; protected
the frontiers of the west Union from invasion, which may in some
measure compensate the people there for the disappointment of
dissolving it; these unions were not dissolved without severe struggles and resentment from those who were thereby debarred a seat
in the Legislature.

The neglect of Congress in admitting Vermont into the federal
union, agreeable to their plighted faith in their resolves of the 7th
and 20th of August, enforced by the weight of the character of the
Commander in Chief of their armies, was a deviation from that candour and honour that ever ought to influence the Representatives
of a free people: they also sacrificed the honour of their General,
so far as in them lay; for it is to be supposed he had been con-
225 sulted by them, as the bearer of the resolve of Congress of
the 7th of August had also a verbal message from him, as before stated; this also gave great reason to suppose, that said resolves were passed through fear, and that the completion of the
matters and engagements therein contained, were procrastinated
through resentment, party intrigues, Jesuitical cunning, and little-
ness; for there could be no necessity of evasive policy, at a time
when the public sentiment called for the discussion of a question
which had already occasioned so much trouble, anxiety, and danger to the United States, and the right of the people of Vermont
to be admitted a sister State into the union was acknowledged
by a great majority of the citizens; consequently, every thing was
prepared for the admission of Vermont into the federal union, but
the interest of the New York land-jobbers; and they made a most
egregious blunder, that they did not seize the opportunity of popular divisions in the Legislature of Vermont, and induce her delegates to have signed the confederacy of the United States; thereby
to have extended the laws of the United States over Vermont,
without any stipulation respecting the grants of land made by the
late colony of New York; in which case they would have probably saved to themselves about 2,500,000 acres of land, that were
granted by the late colony of New York on Crown lands, and afterwards granted by the Legislature of Vermont; for, in a legal
sense, suppose a Court, under the same circumstances as the pres-
226 ent Circuit Court of the United States, then suppose a cause
on the title of lands, where a grant is made in 1768 by the
late colony of New York, by express authority from his Majesty
and Privy Council; then, a subsequent grant from the Legislature
of Vermont. If the Court would decide in favour of the first grant
on Crown lands, then the precipitate act of the Legislature in dissolving

solving her unions, dissolved most of the grants of land that she
had made; but a blind fate, in hardening the hearts of Congress,
(and not the wisdom of the Legislature) saved her citizens from
the loss of these lands, and joining the confederacy, at a time when
it would have involved them in a share of the continental debt.
Nevertheless, she lost a great part of the retaliation on her old adversary, New York, (which was dear to some) the west union, and
with that extensive tract of vacant lands and confiscated estates,
that might have been preserved to enrich her citizens.

That the reader may have full information of the measures made
use of to render null and void all the grants of land made by the
late colony of New York, within the State of Vermont, it is necessary to make a concise statement of the proceedings.——The Legislature early appointed Mr. Ira Allen Surveyor General, in order
to ascertain their vacant lands; measures were taken to grant
lands as early as 1779; as the original object of some of the founders of the State was to overturn all the titles of lands
227 granted by New York. The Surveyor General entered no
grants on his chart but those made by the province of New Hampshire and the State of Vermont, and appeared to have little knowledge of the grants made by New York, till it was found some
grants interfered with those made by New York: in one or two
instances a deduction was made on that account, in the granting
fees; but the current of opposition was so great to New York,
that but little attention was paid to the claims of New York: the
repeated applications for grants of land from the citizens of Vermont and the neighbouring States were such, that soon after the
close of the war, all the lands in the State, except those granted
by New Hampshire, were granted by Vermont, and measures were
taken to settle the same, in order to which, the Legislature proceeded to enact laws to ascertain and establish town-lines; this
became essentially necessary, to prevent settlement on grants made
under New York. Every exertion was made to carry these matters into effect. Different interests, parties, intrigues for popularity, &c. obstructed these measures, and prevented the Surveyor
General from collecting taxes for running town-lines; but, by advice of the Governor and Council, he continued the survey, by
advancing the necessary supplies till the claimants under Vermont
could find all their lands that were attempted to be settled under
New-York titles. ˙ By these exertions, and the spirit of the people,
in opposition to the claims of New York, there were no claims of
228 people settled on lands in Vermont, under titles from New
York, to prevent a settlement between the Commissioners of
New York and Vermont in 1790, when it was stipulated, that the
State

State of Vermont should pay to the State of New York 30,000 dollars, as an equivalent and extirpation for all the titles of land derived from the late colony of New York within the State of Vermont, amounting to about 5,000,000 acres of land, near one half of which was made on Crown lands, never granted by the late province of New Hampshire, and might probably have been considered legal titles, had not the settlement aforesaid rendered them null and void.

The founders of Vermont are justified by the following statement, to some who may feel themselves aggrieved by the loss of property, in setting aside said grants from New York, which in one sense might have been considered legal, so far as they did not interfere with the grants from New Hampshire; but when it is considered that the original object of the Cabinet Council in the colony of New York, in obtaining the order of his Majesty and Privy Council, on the 20th day of July, 1764, extending the colony of New York to the west banks of Connecticut River, was to overturn the titles of land granted by the province of New Hampshire, and subject the inhabitants to be tenants to the land monopolists of New York, which fully appears in the preceding part of this history, and a few remarks in this place will evince 229 the Governor and Council of New York, in issuing their grants, paid no deference to the ancient grants from the province of New Hampshire, which was also a Royal Government. Great part of the grants made by the Governor and Council were illegal, as being opposed to an express prohibition of the King and Privy Council. The supreme Court of New York, in case of a writ of ejectment, would not allow a charter under the great seal of the province of New Hampshire to be read in court, as evidence of title to lands; gave judgment and writs of possession against the proprietors and settlers under New Hampshire. Mr. Kemp, King's Attorney for the colony of New York, on obtaining said judgment, observed to the agent of the people of the district of the New Hampshire Grants, that "might often overcomes right;" he therefore advised the people on the New Hampshire Grants to make the best terms they could with their landlords under New York. That this was an unprovoked attack on the part of the New-York claimants against an innocent people, to take from them that which they had acquired by the sweat of their brow, who resisted, and after a spirited controversy of 26 years, wrested from the claimants under New York about the same number of acres of lands as the New-York claimants had in cold blood, without the least provocation, sought occasion and attempted to take from the New Hampshire claimants; that, after all this, the people of Vermont,

mont, for the sake of good neighbourhood, paid, for the benefit of
230 the New York claimants, 30,000 dollars. This conduct of the
citizens of Vermont (when properly understood) will be jus-
tied both in heaven and on earth, yet it may be hard on some individuals, claiming under New York; but the blame must rest on
the late colony of New York.

In the spring of 1782, a loyalist officer, out of Canada, having
raised seventeen recruits in the county of Albany, State of New
York, set out to conduct them to Canada; he supposed it was
safer to pass through Vermont than to continue in the State of
New York; they were furnished with some stores at the roaring
branch in Arlington. As they were putting them into their knap-
sacks in the silent watches of the night, Lieutenant William Blanchard passing that way, fell in amongst them; they made a prisoner
of him. On their march to Canada, they fell in also with Serjeant
Ormsbury, who shared the same fate with Blanchard. To prevent
alarm, they struck off the road immediately, and took to the woods.
The next morning early, Major Ormsbury was apprized of the situation of his son and his fellow-prisoner, and the route the enemy
had taken. The Major dispatched an express to Colonel Ira
Allen, to inform him of this circumstance, as the Colonel at that
time commanded a regiment of militia in that neighbourhood. In
the mean time, the Major directed Captain Sunderland to pursue
the enemy with a party of men. The Captain took his hounds
231 with him, who, by their scent followed the tracks of the
enemy, and thus proved faithful guides to the party.

Colonel Allen, on the receipt of this intelligence, posted full
speed to Manchester, sent to Captain Eastman, of Ruport, directing him to raise a party of men, and way-lay in a certain pass in
the mountain, where he took the said recruiting party, and released
Lieutenant Blanchard. Captain Sunderland came up in a few moments after, when the sagacity of his hounds was amazingly per-
ceptible, by going up and smelling to the feet of the prisoners, who
were brought to Sunderland; the Governor, General Ethan Allen,
&c. attended their examination. A simple, honest-looking fellow
was the first examined, and whilst the attention of the populace
was drawn to hear it, an officer, that was in the secret, found
means to let the prisoners know, that they must call themselves
British soldiers, in a loyalist corps, when it was discovered that
the recruiting officer had his recruiting orders, enlistments, &c.
with him, which he was directed immediately to destroy, as the
price

price of their lives; they were examined, considered as prisoners, of war, and sent to Bennington gaol.

Colonel Ira Allen wrote to the British Commissioners in Canada, informing them of these matters, requiring about double the number of prisoners in exchange; that such measures might give satisfaction to the people of Vermont, and this requisition was complied with.

232

In the mean time a strong party, in and about Bennington, who were opposed to any negociation with the British, threatened to oppose the said prisoners being sent to Canada in exchange. The Governor being informed of this, and that the party was gaining strength, directed a spirited officer, with a number of men, to repair to Bennington, to take the prisoners out of confinement, and march them to the frontiers, for the purpose of being carteled, which he did.

Colonel Warner, and a Committee, came from Bennington to Governor Chittenden's, where a warm altercation took place, as the gentlemen from Bennington disputed the propriety of the conduct of the Governor, in sending the prisoners to the northward, and threatened to raise a regiment of men to bring them back. Governor Chittenden answered, that he had not taken this step 'till he had consulted the Council, and so done what he thought proper, and should not recall the orders he had given respecting said prisoners, and did not doubt but Colonel Allen's regiment, who had taken said prisoners, were sufficient to support his orders in opposition to any measure they could take; that they might depend that the northern part of the State united in opinion with him and the Council; he therefore coolly advised them to return to Bennington, and persuade the people to be quiet; that they would soon see a generous return of prisoners from Canada; the dispute subsided, and in a short time forty prisoners were returned, part of whom were citizens of the United States. Nevertheless, Major Fay, as Commissary of prisoners, receipted them; when these matters were known, opposition ceased, and the conduct of the Governor was approved by all parties.

233

Early in 1782, men were directed to be raised for the defence of the frontiers of Vermont, and each town to furnish its quota; opposition was made to these measures in the south east part of the State, through the intrigues of New York; indeed that State went so far as to issue commissions, which, with other measures, produced an armed force within Vermont, to oppose her laws; five

of

of the principal offenders were taken, and brought before the supreme Court; the laws of Vermont were established on wisdom and moderation, which admitted acts of treasonable offences to be punished by banishment and confiscation of estates; sentences to this effect were passed, and executed on the offenders; complaint was made by the Government of New York to Congress, predicated on the resolves of that body, Sept. 24, 1779, and June 2d, 1780. Congress took up the complaint, and referred it to a Committee, who, on the 14th of November, reported, "that the measures complained of were probably occasioned by the State of New York having lately issued commissions, both civil and military, to 234 persons resident in the district called Vermont:" And that it be recommended to New York, to revoke all the commissions which they had issued since the month of May; that it be recommended to the inhabitants to make full satisfaction to the persons who had suffered damages; and that it be recommended to New York, and to the people exercising Government in Vermont, to adhere to the resolutions of Congress, of September 24th, until a decision should be had upon their affairs. But after several attempts, a vote could not be obtained in favor of these resolves, and the matter was adjourned.*

On December 5th, 1782, these matters were again attended to by Congress, in violation of solemn faith, pledged to Vermont in their resolves of the 7th and 20th of August, assuming a power not vested in them, by attempting to controul the internal police of Vermont, as by the following resolves will appear.

" By the United States in Congress assembled, December 5, 1782 : Whereas it appears to Congress, by authentic documents, that the people inhabiting the district of country, on the west side of Connecticut River, commonly called the New Hampshire Grants, and claiming to be an independent State, in contempt of the authority of Congress, and in direct violation of their resolutions of the 24th of September, 1779, and of the 2d of June, 235 1780, did, in the month of September last, proceed to exercise jurisdiction over the persons and properties of sundry inhabitants of the said district, professing themselves to be the subjects of, and to owe allegiance to the State of New York; by means whereof divers of them have been condemned to banishment, not to return on pain of death and confiscation of estate, and others have been fined in large sums, and otherwise deprived of property. Therefore, resolved, that the said acts and proceedings of the said people, being highly derogatory to the authority of the United States,

* Journal of Congress, November 14, 1782.

and

and dangerous to the confederacy, require the immediate and decided interposition of Congress, for the protection and relief of such
as have suffered by them, and for preserving peace in the said district, until a decision shall be had of the controversy relative to
the jurisdiction of the same.

" That the people inhabiting the said district claiming to be independent, be, and they are hereby required without delay to
make full and ample restitution to Timothy Church, Timothy
Phelps, Henry Evans, William Shattuck, and such others, as have
been condemned to banishment and confiscation of estates, or have
otherwise been deprived of property, since the first day of September last, for the damages they have sustained by the acts and proceedings aforesaid, and that they be not molested in their
236 persons or properties, on their return to their habitations in
the said district.

" That the United States will take effectual measures to enforce a compliance with the aforesaid resolutions, in case the same
shall be disobeyed by the people of the said district."

The people of Vermont were already prejudiced against the
proceedings of Congress; these resolutions could not fail to im-
pair all that remained of reverence and respect. The Governor
and Council sent a spirited remonstrance to Congress against these
resolutions.* In this remonstrance Congress was reminded of
their solemn engagements to the State of Vermont, in their public
acts of August 7th, and 20th, 1781, which had been fully complied
with on the part of the State, but which Congress had refused or
neglected to fulfil : They were told that by their own articles of
confederation, they had no right to interfere or meddle with
the internal police of any of the United States ; and least of all
with that of Vermont, from which they had not received any delegated authority whatever : That Vermont had as good a right to
independence as Congress ; and as much authority to pass resolutions prescribing measures to Congress, as Congress had to prescribe measures, directing them to receive the banished, and
237 make restitution to criminals of the property which had been
taken from them by due course of law, for their crimes against the
laws and authority of the State : They were reminded that they
were pursuing the same measures against Vermont, which Britain
had used against the American colonies, and which it had been
judged necessary to oppose at every risk and hazard : That their

* January 9, 1783.

proceedings

proceedings tended to make the liberty and natural rights of mankind a mere bubble, and the sport of state politicians : That it was of no importance to America to pull down arbitrary power in one form, that they might establish it in another : That the inhabitants of Vermont had lived in a state of independence from the first settlement of the country, and could not now submit to be resolved out of it by the influence which New York, their old adversary, had in Congress : That they were in full possession of freedom, and would remain independent, notwithstanding all the power and artifice of New York : That they had no controversy with the United States, complexly considered ; but were at all times ready and able to vindicate their rights and liberties, against the usurpations of the State of New York.

With regard to that part of the resolves, which declared " the proceedings of Vermont to be derogatory to the authority of the United States, and dangerous to the confederacy, and such as required the immediate interposition of Congress to relieve the sufferers, and preserve peace," they answer, that it appears like a paradox to assert that the exercise of civil law in Vermont should be derogatory to the authority or dangerous to the confederacy of the United States ; or that the interposition of Congress would be the means of establishing peace in the State.   Law, justice, and order, they assert, were established in Vermont, before Congress passed their late resolutions ; what discord they would occasion, time would determine : But that it was the general opinion that a ratification of their stipulated agreement, would have had a more salutary tendency to promote peace, than their late resolutions.

238

As to the requisition that " the State without delay make full and ample restitution to those who had been condemned to banishment and confiscation of estate," they observe, that Congress has been so mutable in their resolutions respecting Vermont, that it is impossible to know on what ground to find them, or what they design next.   At one time they guarantee to the States of New Hampshire and New York, their lands to certain described limits, leaving a place for the existence of the State of Vermont ; the next thing Vermont hears from them, is, they are within these limits controlling the internal Government of the State.   Again, they prescribe preliminaries of confederation, and when complied with on the part of the State, they unreasonably procrastinate the ratification.

To

239   To that part of the resolves in which the State was threatened, " that the United States would take effectual measures to enforce a compliance with their resolutions, in case they should be disobeyed by the people of said district," they return for answer that the State would appeal to the justice of his Excellency General Washington; and as the General and most of the inhabitants of the contiguous States, were in favour of the independence of Vermont, it would be more prudent for Congress to refer the settlement of this dispute to the States of New York and Vermont, than to embroil the confederacy with it. But supposing Congress had a judicial authority to controul the internal police of the State, the State had a right to be heard in its defence. That the proceedings of Congress were wholly unjustifiable, upon their own principles; and that coming to a decision of so important a matter, *ex parte*, and without any notice to the State, was illegal, and contrary to the law of nature and nations. The remonstrance was concluded with soliciting a federal union with the United States, agreeable to their preliminary agreement, which their Committee had reported was " become *absolute* and *necessary* on their part to be peformed; " and from which, they were assured, Vermont would not recede.

The Assembly met in the month of February, and sent their remonstrance to Congress. Like that of the Governor and Council, this was also plain, spirited, and decisive; announcing to Congress, in the plainest terms, that they should not intermeddle in the internal affairs of Government; and that they were fully resolved to maintain their independence.

240

These resolves, instead of intimidating the people of Vermout, united them in a spirited opposition; the Legislature annually appointed agents and delegates to Congress, but took no further pains to join the confederacy; indeed they found themselves in better circumstances than those of the neighbouring States, on account of taxes, and were content with the measures of Government.

In the winter of 1782, the British in Canada were impatient to learn what effect the capture of Lord Cornwallis had produced. Their anxiety and confidence in the people of Vermont, will best appear from the stile in the extract of the following letter from the British agent, dated February 28th, 1782. " My anxiety to hear from you, induced me to apply to his Excellency (General Haldimand) for leave to send the bearer with this; which having obtained, I earnestly request you to send me, in the most candid, unreserved

unreserved manner, the present wishes and intentions of the people, and leading men of your State, respecting our former negociations ; and what effect the late catastrophe of Lord Cornwallis has on them. Will it not be well to consider the many chances and vicissitudes of war? However brilliant the last campaign may appear, the next may wear a very different aspect: Add to this, the great probability of your being ruined by your haughty neighbours, elated by (what they call) a signal victory; and I hope you will see, as I do, that it is more than ever your interest, to unite yourselves with those who wish to make you a happy and free Government. Will there be a proper time to send the proclamations? I repeat my request, that you will tell me, without reserve, what may be expected in future."

241

April 22d, 1782, the British agents wrote, " in confidence, we take this opportunity to acquaint you, by the authority of his Excellency General Haldimand, that he is still inclined to treat amicably with the people of Vermont; and these his generous and humane inclinations, are now seconded by much stronger powers from his Majesty, than he has hitherto enjoyed for that purpose. We do, in confidence, officially assure you, that every article proposed to you in his Excellency's former offer, as well as the confirmation of the east and west unions, in their utmost limits, will be amply and punctually complied with. We hope your answer may be such, as to unburden our anxious minds." Extremely fearful about the event, and impatient at not receiving an answer, on April 30th they wrote again, and carried their offers and promises to a still greater extent: " His Excellency has never lost sight of his first object ; and I am happy to be able in this, to inform you, that the General has lately received, by way of Halifax, full powers from the King to establish V————t Government, including the full extent of the east and west unions, with every privilege and immunity, formerly proffered to you; and he is likewise fully authorized, as well as sincerely inclined, to provide amply for *****, and to make ***** Brigadier General in the line, ********** field officers, with such other rewards, as your sincerity, and good services in bringing about the revolution, may in future merit. In short, the General is vested with full powers to make such rewards, as he shall judge proper, to all those who distinguish themselves in promoting the happy union: And as his Excellency has the greatest confidence in you, and *****, much will depend on your recommendations."

242

Extract

Extract from General Haldimand's Letter in the Summer of 1782.

" You may rest assured that I shall give such orders, as will effectually prevent hostilities of any kind being exercised in the district of Vermont, until such time as a breach on your part, or some general event, may make the contrary my duty. And you have my authority to promulgate, in such manner as you shall think fit, this my intention to the people of the said district, that they may, without any apprehension, continue to encourage and 243 promote the settlement and cultivation of that new country, to the interest and happiness of themselves, and their posterity." *

One of the British agents wrote, March 25th, 1783, after some reports of peace, and before officially made known, in this stile :

" I am commanded to acquaint you, that actuated from the beginning, by a sincere desire of serving you, and your people, as well as of promoting the royal cause, by re-uniting you with the mother country, his Excellency never lost an opportunity of representing every circumstance that could be advanced in your favour, to the King's Ministers, in the hope of accomplishing a reconciliation. His Excellency will continue by such representations, to do all in his power to serve you, but what effect it may have, at this late period, is very uncertain. While his Excellency sincerely regrets the happy moment, which it is much to be feared, cannot be recalled, of restoring to you the blessings of the British Government, and views with concern the fatal consequences approaching, which he has so long, and so frequently predicted, from your procrastination, he derives some satisfaction from a consciousness of not having omitted a circumstance, which could 244 tend to your persuasion, and adoption of his desired purpose. In the present uncertain state of affairs, uninformed as his Excellency is, of what is doing, or perhaps done, in a general accommodation, he does not think fit, until the result shall be known, to give any opinion, which may influence you, perhaps, to the prejudice of your interests, or that might interfere with the views of Government. If the report now prevailing has any foundation, a very short time will determine the fate of Vermont. Should any thing favourable present, you may still depend on his Excellency's utmost endeavours, for your salvation."

* Haldimand's letter to Governor Chittenden, dated Quebec, 8th August, 1782.

                                                                    The

The preceding letter, under the circumstances it was written, shews the generous conduct of General Haldimand, in the course of these negociations, and a friendly liberality in cautioning the people of Vermont to be on their guard for new events. The facts are, that these negociations, on the part of Vermont, were from necessity, as has been already shewn; on the part of the British, they were to carry into effect the object of the war; from different motives those measures were carried on in such ways as the parties could agree for their mutual interest, on the strictest principles of honor; and when peace was proclaimed, impressions of friendship remained between the parties, as several interviews between General Haldimand and Colonel Ira Allen afterwards fully evinced.

245   In January, 1783, the late Colonel Samuel Wells, of Brattleborough, being engaged in transmitting letters from Canada to New York, one of his packets was intercepted, and fell into the hands of some of the officers of the continental troops. In consequence of which, a Captain, with a company from Albany, were dispatched to seize the Colonel; who, on being informed of this circumstance, left his house, to take shelter in Canada. In his flight he put up at Captain Otly's, at Bromley, in the Green Mountains; while at supper the Captain and his men came to the house, and put up for the night. Notwithstanding Colonel Wells was fully apprized of the Captain's business, reflecting that there was no dwelling at hand to which he could escape, such an attempt, besides, might awaken suspicions in the Captain, who was about to retire to rest, the Colonel went to bed, and remained there till his pursuers set out to Brattleborough, in hopes to find him there. Colonel Wells proceeded to Sunderland, to consult with General and Colonel Allen, who advised him to set out for New York about twelve o'clock at night; a sleigh was accordingly provided for that purpose, which was brought to General Allen's door at the appointed hour; he set out in it, and having pursued his instructions, in the course of a few nights he arrived at New York in safety.

On the news of peace in 1783, between Great Britain and the United States, finding that the territory of Vermont was in-
246   cluded within the boundaries of the latter as relinquished by the former, the Governor and Council appointed Colonel Ira Allen their Commissioner, to concert measures with the Legislative Council of Canada for opening a free commercial intercourse with that province; but the most essential part of his mission was to confer with the Commander in Chief, General Haldimand, with respect

respect to the views of the British Government, as applied to Vermont in particular, and the United States in general. It is to be observed, that many propositions had passed between the agents of Great Britain and Vermont, respecting Vermont's being a colony under the crown of England; that by the preliminaries of peace Vermont was within the territory conceded to the United States as aforesaid; that she had dissolved her unions with them, a part of her consequence, and was not received into the confederacy of the United States. In this situation, completely independent, and not in alliance or connexion with any power on earth, she had cautiously avoided contracting much debt; therefore wisdom dictated moderation, that she might take advantage of whatever circumstances should arise from the new order of things; that considering the multiplied debts the United States had contracted, in the course of their struggles for independence; that their constitution had not sufficient energy to govern an extensive country in time of peace; consequently a new constitution would be 247 necessary in the United States, the formation and ratification of which, the liquidation and settlement of the public accounts, providing ways and means for discharging the same, were respectively arduous tasks; and the more so, when it was considered that the sense of danger from without gave rise to new discords within, and between the States a difference in political sentiments and interests might be difficult to reconcile. What influence British agents would have, or what their objects might be, in the United States, under these circumstances, was also a question. Under these impressions, the Governor and Council of Vermont instructed Colonel Ira Allen, at different times, to repair to Quebec, to confer with Governor Haldimand, his successor, &c. on the preceding matters, and to advise for the best good of Vermont; the result of which was, that it was adviseable for Vermont to consolidate the interest of her citizens, on one common principle, and admit of no titles to lands, but those derived from New Hampshire, their subsequent confirmations, on the same grounds, from New York, that were in some instances made near Connecticut River, and the Grants made by Vermont; and to form no connexions with the United States for the time being, or until the United States should establish a more permanent constitution, liquidate and provide ways and means for the discharge of their debts. This policy being adopted by certain persons in Vermont, was steadily pursued by them. When the insurrection arose in the neighbouring State of Massachusett's, headed by Mr. Shays, some 248 time before the insurgents attempted to take the arsenal of the United States at Springfield, Mr. Shays sent Luke Day and Eli Parsons, two of his officers, to General Ethan Allen, Commandant

mandant of the militia of Vermont, offering him (General Allen) the command of the revolutionary army, or insurgents of the Massachusett's; which General Ethan Allen contemptuously refused, directing said men to leave the State of Vermont. General Allen then wrote to the Governor of Massachusett's, stating the circumstance, assuring him that no asylum would be given in the State of Vermont to the insurgents of the State of Massachusett's. General Lincoln sent Major Royal Tylor, one of his aid-du-camps, to the Legislature of Vermont, the October following, to further confirm these measures, and to cultivate a good understanding between the States of Massachusett's and Vermont, who received every satisfaction he could have expected from the Legislature.

After the ratification of the Constitution of the United States, in 1788, Congress convened in New York. Federal Hall was dedicated to the use of Congress, at a great expence of the citizens, and measures were taking to remove Congress to Philadelphia. The citizens of New York, considering Vermont to be too firmly established to expect to overturn the government, or get possession of the lands granted by the late colony of New York, proposed the admission of Vermont into the federal government, in order to which the Legislature of the State of New York 249 passed an act, appointing Commissioners, with full powers to settle boundary lines, and all disputes respecting lands, between the States of New York and Vermont. The Legislature of Vermont passed an act, appointing Commissioners with similar powers, to settle boundary lines, &c.

The aforesaid Commissioners, after several meetings, established the boundaries of jurisdiction, as they then were exercised by said States. All titles to lands within the bounds of Vermont, that derived from the late colony of New York, were annulled, except some in confirmation of the New Hampshire Grants, contiguous to Connecticut River. As compensation for the loss of these lands, the State of Vermont stipulated and paid to the State of New York 30,000 Spanish milled dollars. These acts of said Commissioners were ratified and confirmed by the Legislature of the States of New York and Vermont; in virtue of which, writs of election were then issued by the Governor, directing the freemen of each town to elect members for a Convention, who were to convene for the purpose of first determining whether they would resolve to come into the confederacy of the United States, and if so, to approve, disapprove, or make proposed amendments to the Constitution of the United States. In three days after the convening of such Convention, they resolved to come into the confederacy

federacy of the United States, and approved of their Constitution by an almost unanimous vote.

250   The Legislature of Vermont passed an act, appointing Nathaniel Chipman and Lewis R. Morris, Esquires, with full powers to negociate the admission of Vermont into the federal union, and sign the confederation of the United States, which was done, making the settlement with New York the basis of the admission of Vermont into the federal government ; so that 30,000 dollars, with good management, cancelled grants from the late colony of New York, for about 5,000,000 acres of land, after a spirited dispute of twenty-six years.

In 1791, the Honorable Moses Robinson and Stephen R. Bradley, Esquires, as senators, Nathaniel Niles and Israel Smith, Esquires, as representatives of Vermont, took their seats in Congress.

The first settlers of Vermont laboured under great disadvantages in educating their children, for want of proper schools; yet, nevertheless, care was taken to instruct them to read and write in the English language, and so much in arithmetic as to do any common business, and keep accounts. There is scarcely a man in the State that cannot do this, or a female that cannot read and write. These difficulties have in a great measure subsided, except in the new settlements.

In the townships granted by the Governor of New Hampshire, one right of land, containing about 340 acres, was reserved for 251 the use of schools in each township ; one right was reserved for the propagation of the Gospel in foreign parts, which, by an act of the Legislature in October, 1794, was also appropriated to the use of town schools.

In the townships granted by Vermont, there was one right reserved for town schools, and one right for county grammar schools. It has been proposed to appropriate the right from grammar schools to town schools, which would make two rights in each township through the State for town schools. From the avails of these lands, and other measures, a sufficient number of schools will be erected to give early instruction to the youth of Vermont. Several academies are established in different parts of the State, with handsome funds for their support, by benefactions of their founders.

Dartmouth

Dartmouth College, established by the late reverend and learned Doctor Eleazer Whelock, took its name from the liberal benefaction of the Earl of Dartmouth, is situated in Hanover, in the State of New Hampshire, near the east bank of Connecticut River, to which the Legislature of Vermont gave a township of land, six miles square ; which College is well endowed and organized, and is one of the most flourishing in the United States, under the presidency of the Honourable John Whelock, LL. D.

252   Williams College, so called in commemoration of its founder and benefactor, Colonel Williams, is established in Williamstown, near the south-west corner of Vermont, which has been lately organized, and is in respectable circumstances, increasing fast in its numbers of students and reputation, under the presidency of the Honourable Doctor Fitch.

The university of Vermont was established at Burlington Bay, on the east bank of Lake Champlain, in 1791, in pursuance of a memorial of Ira Allen, Esq; to the Legislature in 1789, and on the following benefactions :——

By Ira Allen, Esq; -	£4,000 0 0
By his Excellency Governor Chittenden -	300 0 0
By General Spafford - - - - -	200 0 0
By William Coit, Esq; - - - - -	200 0 0

Which, with donations of gentlemen in and near Burlington, increased the benefactions to nearly £10,000. Besides the gifts of the above individuals, the Legislature endowed the university with a right of land in each township, granted by them, the total amount of which is about fifty thousand acres.

The trustees appointed by the Legislature are gentlemen of different religious sentiments, to prevent any kind of preference being given to religious or political parties. They have cordially
253   united in promoting the true interest of the university, by leasing out the lands, in the first place, rather than appropriate the capital in buildings, and organizing said university, except that part of the donations, consisting of materials, which have been employed in erecting public buildings.

From the funds appropriated to schools, academies, colleges, and universities, in and contiguous to Vermont; from the disposition of the people to contribute further to support those institutions, and desire to extend knowledge amongst all orders, great benefits may be expected to rising generations.

The

The Legislatnre of Vermont, in October, 1794, passed an act, authorising the select men of each town to lease the glebe right, and annually to apply the avails in support of the minister or ministers of the respective towns, in proportion to their hearers, without giving preference to any religious denomination, as all sects are equally countenanced by the laws of Vermont.

The liberal grants of land in the several towns within the State to support religious worship, will, no doubt, highly advance society, and be the means of teaching people to pay the tribute of adoration due to the Author of Nature, which ought to be regarded by all communities for present and future benefits.

254 The situation of Vermont for commerce may be judged of by Captain Twist's estimate of the expence of a canal sufficient for a ship of 200 tons to pass from the River St. Lawrance into Lake Champlain for £27,000 sterling, as noted in page 4, and a canal that is now nearly completed from navigable waters in Hudson's River, sufficient to pass boats of 25 tons burthen into said lake, which is further elucidated by the prefixed map. The inland canals, which may be extended through most of Vermont, the fertility of the country, the variety of raw materials and uncultivated lands for want of inhabitants, point out mutual advantages, with a manufacturing nation to supply many articles for convenience and luxury ; that by the treaty of 1794, British ships are allowed to navigate the waters of Lake Champlain for the purpose of commerce, and to render said waters useful and interesting to both nations, the canal ought to be completed, and the shipping of Vermont permitted to pass Quebec, on paying a trifling acknowledgment ; or, as an equivalent for British ships navigating the waters of said lake. Were these plans accomplished, they would be more interesting to Great Britain than to the United States, and the merchants need not be further told how to take the advantage thereof.

The Government of Vermont admits not of hereditary powers, nor democracy, nor aristocracy, but is founded on the principle of 255 representation. By its constitution, the people retain the right of annually convening in their respective towns, to give their votes for a Governor, Deputy Governor, 12 Counsellors, and to chuse a representative for each town, who afterwards meet and form " The General Assembly of the State of Vermont," which Assembly so convened enact laws by the power derived from the people, to whom the Assembly is responsible. This system of Government seems to be founded in nature and true policy ; and
most

most likely will be supported by reason and self-preservation, because every man has equal rights to lose and defend with his
neighbours, and expects safety, wealth, and preferment, according
to his virtues, abilities, and talents.

The General Assembly is impowered to appoint Judges, Sheriffs, and Magistrates, as well as Major Generals and Brigadier
Generals; but the Governor and Council commission them and
all other military officers.

The General Assembly have, by their delegated power, divided
the State into eleven counties, and appointed Judges, Sheriffs, and
Justices of the Peace. The militia have been formed into companies of infantry, artillery, cavalry, regiments, brigades, and four
divisions. Their numbers in 1781 were estimated to be 7,000;
in 1792 they were computed to be 18,500; and in 1798 they may
be near 30,000.

256 The annual expences of the Government of Vermont, from
October 1, 1791, to October 1, 1792, amounted to £3,219 9s.
9d. currency, that is, reckoning a guinea at 28s. and the expences
have not generally differed since.

The revenue of the State depends not on commerce, but on taxation of real and personal property. In 1791, the whole *list* of
the taxable property of the State amounted to £324,796 18s. 10d;
when the sum of expence, in 1791 was divided between the inhab-
tants of the State, according to the census, it was found that each
person paid only six-pence three farthings to Government for the
protection of his *person, liberty,* and *property.*

It may be difficult to find any part of the civilized world, where
the inhabitants enjoy the protection and blessings of Government
at so little expence as the people of Vermont.

The population of Vermont, taken by the census in 1792,
amounted to 85,589, which number has been greatly enlarged
since from migrations and births. It appears that the climate of
Vermont is salubrious and healthy, from the bills of mortality
inserted in the history written by *Dr. Williams*, page 367, for the
years 1789, 1790, 1791: the number of inhabitants then in Rutland was 1407—Deaths 47—Births 223; and in other towns
the ratio of deaths and births were similar; it thence appears,
257 that deaths in Vermont, compared with the births, were in
proportion of 1 to 4; therefore, without including the migrations

grations into the State, the people will naturally double their numbers in nineteen years and five months, " While in Great Britain and most other countries in Europe, they are not supposed to double in less time than five hundred years." * From this comparative natural increase of the human race in Vermont, with that of most parts of Europe, we are apt to inquire for the causes, which are, either the climates, the civil forms of Government, the luxury of the rich, the extreme poverty of the poor, long bloody wars, large fleets and numerous armies, the servitude of the peasants, the impious law of celibacy, or a feudal system pervading the old world, where the natual increase of mankind is uncertain and very slow.

Machiavelian policy has been long celebrated, though it has been as long destroying the noblest productions of nature, the rapid increase of people, the strength, prosperity, and wealth of nations.

* Smith's Wealth of Nations, Vol. 1, page 94.

APPENDIX

S I R ,

258 I received your queries, and am glad to have it in my power to answer them, and I hope to your satisfaction, for I know you are one of the few that looks for nothing beyond truth and plain language. As I sent you an accurate map of Vermont, it is needless to repeat the situation of it ; a map, it is true, may be dressed out in gaudy colours, and a writer, of a warm imagination, may embellish the most barren country; but there is no occasion for any aids of this kind in treating of the present subject, it will be sufficient to state things as they are, and I promise you that I will not exceed the limits of truth.——I need not tell you that I have travelled through some of the finest countries of Europe, and paused with rapture on some of the most picturesque views, and I do not hesitate to say that Vermont vies with many of them even in her present state.   Pere Martini,* who lived many years in Canada, and visited this country, says that Vermont may be called one of the daughters of Columbia; but what would he say if he saw it at present, abounding with scenes that would charm the eye and gladden the heart ? for what can be more pleasing to a benevolent mind, than to see a hardy race, with nerves strong by

259 labour and complexions ruddy with industry, cultivating the grateful soil, tending their flocks, or employed at intervals in the discharge of domestic duties, sensible of the blessings of rational liberty, and the sweets of seasonable repose.

You see by the map that a chain of lofty mountains extends from the north to the south, and divides the State nearly in the middle, hence it has obtained its name from the French word *Verdmont,* and never was a name more applicable, for even in winter they are cloathed with verdure, and crowned with lofty woods.   The contrast betwixt the cultivated and uncultivated grounds is exceedingly pleasing, and even inviting to the labour of the husbandman.   In this contrast he sees the effect of his own powers, aided by the goodness of providence ; he sees that he can embellish the most rude spot, the stagnant air vanishes with the woods, the rank vegetation feels the purifying influence of the sun ; he drains the swamp, putrid exhalations flit off on lazy wing, and fevers and agues accompany them.   It is true, there is not much occasion for all those efforts in this State, for the climate is healthy, and for the truth of this assertion, I might appeal to the longevity of the inhabitants, many of

* See Martini's Letters, vol. . Paris, 1744.

whom

whom enjoy what the Physicians call the *Youth of Old Age* ; I would
not have said this much if many of the Europeans did not affect to talk
of the sudden transitions of the seasons in this quarter of the globe, and
a long string of attendant diseases, the offspring rather of luxury and
260 debauchery, which I hope will be the last and most unwelcome
visitants in the state. Your third query puzzles me a little, for I
am really at a loss in the classification of the inhabitants—they are all
farmers, and again every farmer is a mechanic in some line or other,
as inclination leads or necessity requires. The hand that guides the
plough frequently constructs it, and the labours of the axe and the plane
often evince a degree of genius and dexterity that would really amaze
you. As to what you call day-labourers the number is few, and if industrious they can soon emerge from that situation, the farmer does not
look down on them with an eye of severity or contempt, on the contrary
he holds out his hand to them, and assists to raise them on a level with
himself. When a new settler arrives, it is not material from what part
of the world he came, industry and a good character are the best recommendations, and if he brings these with him, he is received with hospitality and kindness. A large family is considered as a blessing, for there
is employment and encouragement enough for all. The first thing to be
considered perhaps is a dwelling-house ; this is cheaply and easily rear-
ed, it is composed of timber, as there is plenty of wood ; convenience is
chiefly consulted, the number of rooms is proportioned to the family,
they are well lighted, shingled and airy, though snug and remarkably
clean ; though the furniture is not sumptuous it is useful, and every article is found in its place ; the labours of the family are divided and pro-
261 portioned according to their strength, ingenuity, and sex. Their
diet is wholesome, and the stranger finds a hearty welcome in every
countenance. The little cookery may be said to be hereditary, for there
is scarce a family that has attempted to introduce any luxury in that line,
which their ancestors would be ashamed to see on their table except tea,
on which many now breakfast. Time is divided into labour and rest in-
términgled with innocent amusements, that render the one light and the
other refreshing and sweet ; that the stranger and the traveller may par-
take of their hospitality, the hours of repast are in general fixed and certain ; they breakfast at eight, dine at twelve, and sup at eight. As you
seem to dwell on the day-labourer, I assure you that you would find it
difficult to distinguish betwixt his humble board and the table of the
farmer ; if the former chuses, he can dine on fish, flesh or fowl. What
is the language then that Vermont holds out to persons of this class ?
let us suppose that she addressed them in this manner—" I do not ask
whence you came, nor your religious opinion, you are welcome to enjoy
it ; if you are honest and industrious that is all I ask ; if you can till the
ground, there is a certain portion of it, it will repay your labours ten
fold ; if you want a cottage there is wood at the mere expense of cutting
it

it down, and abundance of fuel. If you want fish, look round, you see
rivers running in every direction, put in your net ; if you want wild fowl
repair to the woods, they'll only cost you powder and shot, there is none
262 to hinder you ; you may rear swine and other domestic animals at an
      easy expence. If you are contented with the fleece in its native colour,
your wife can spin and weave it, and after a few years labour you can
purchase a farm in fee simple, and enjoy the sweets of it ; if your family
is large you can provide for all ; the fruits of your industry is guarded
by wholesome laws, and if you pay a proper respect to them you will be
respected in your turn ; thus you see you can plant a tree, and your
children's children can repose under the shade of it. If such is the state
and prospect of the peasant, what is the situation of the farmer—the
Lord of his own soil, remote from the thunder of power, the false
blandishments of luxury, the glare of unwieldly wealth ; if he knows how
to appreciate the real blessings of life, I know of none that may be called
happier. With respect to the face of the country, if you ask me merely
with regard to rural views, I can say that the landscape painter would be
highly charmed, as I know of no country that abounds in a greater diver-
sity of hill and dale, but I must add that those hills are in general capable
of being converted into arable ground, and that the most craggy mountain
if cleared, would produce tolerable pasturage ; some parts may be compared to the sea in a storm, and others in a gentle breeze ; the plains in
some places extend several miles, particularly along the banks of Lake
Champlain, as you may see by the name. You ask me if the Vermontese
263 are good agriculturists ? I answer that putting everything together
      they have made a rapid progress in that useful branch of science ;
time and opportunity it is true, have not enabled them to make many
Georgical experiments, nor have they occasion, as the soil, with a little
cultivation, furnishes them with all the necessaries of life in abundance,
such as wheat, oats, rye, beans, barley, &c.; they have no necessity to introduce foreign grasses, where every hill and valley affords abundance
of herbage spontaneously, and every plain permitted to remain a few
months untouched becomes a meadow.

I need only give you one instance of the fertility of soil, namely, that
it produces excellent potatoes without manure ; wild hops and grape
vines flourish spontaneously, and arise to such a degree of maturity that
I am persuaded, with the assistance of a little art, they might be brought
to great perfection ; at present the wild grape is only used as a desert,
or to allay thirst, as the taste on that occasion is very agreeable. The
woods also produce other fruits in great plenty, some of which you are
obliged to pamper in your hot-houses in England. If you cast your eye
over the map, you will easily perceive that the country is extremely well
watered. Lake Champlain is a noble chart, and so deep that ships of
war have sailed on it. It is sprinkled with many beautiful, fertile, and
                                                                    well

well inhabited isles, but it is to be lamented that the wealth of its waves should be merely confined to the fisherman, when they might be con-

264 verted to the noblest purposes of trade and useful navigation, for the mutual benefit of millions, by a navigable cut to the river St. Lawrence.

In consequence of an application made by Ira Allen, Esq; of this State, to General Haldiman, Governor of Canada, in 1784 and 1785, the General thought so highly of the proposition, that he appointed Captain Twist, the engineer of that province, to make a survey and estimate the expence of a canal from the river St. Lawrence to Lake Champlain, which was executed in 1785. The Captain began his survey at the rapids of St. John's, and carried it on along the side of the river Sorel to Chamblee, &c. The estimate of the expense of this cut, sufficient to bear vessels of two hundred tons burthen, was calculated at £27,000 sterling. The canal which I now propose is to extend from St. Therese to the river St. Lawrence, as laid down in the map annexed to this book. The expence may exceed the preceding estimate ; but the excess will be amply compensated as the difficulties of a narrow winding river, upwards of thirty miles, would be avoided. It may be necessary to make several surveys to ascertain the best, as the face of the country is level, and the soil marly. The waters of Lake Champlain are higher than the river St. Lawrence, which demonstrate the probability of the measure. It is impossible to

265 calculate the advantages of this undertaking in a commercial point of view ; such an undertaking would promote agriculture, population, arts, manufactures, handicrafts, and all the business of a civilized state, regulated by wise laws, sound policy, a deep sense of religious duty and morality.

To this I shall subjoin the following abstract, taken from General Allen's memorials on this subject, to his Grace the Duke of Portland, &c.—Page 104, Vol. I. of the ship Olive Branch capture.[1]

In an interview with his Grace, General Allen laid down the advantages that would mutually result to the two countries, if such a communication should be carried into effect. His Grace objected to any share of the expence on the part of the British Government, but expressed his readiness to receive, and to consider of proposals for carrying the same into execution on other principles. General Allen, in his Memorials, &c. offered to cut the Canal at his own expence, on condition that he should be secured in a interest of his money, by an order from Government, assigning a tonnage on vessels &c. navigating this Lake, to the amount of said interest ; and that shipping built in said Lake, by the citizens of Vermont, should be permitted to pass to and from the open

---

[1] [See preliminary note *ante.*]

seas,

seas, paying such tonnage as should be deemed reasonable on passing Quebec ; that the manufactures, raw materials, and produce of Vermont, should be permitted to pass to the open sea ; that the manufactures, 266 goods, &c. of Great Britain, should be permitted to be imported in the shipping of Vermont into the said State, without paying any duty oñ such exports or imports, by Act or Acts of the Parliament of Great Britain, or the Legislature of Lower Canada. That contiguous to said Lake was a fertile country, abounding in lumber, iron ore, marble, &c. that the soil produced wheat, Indian corn, peas, barley, hemp, grass, &c. in great abundance ; that the country was erected into a settlement after the conquest of Canada, by the late Lord Amherst, in 1761, and is now estimated at a population of 150,000 souls. That Great Britain, through the medium of the said Canal and Navigation, would, in fact, reap the advantage of the trade of Vermont, and of the northern part of the State of New York, which parts, contiguous to Lake Champlain and Iroquois, would then find it their interest to become a part of the State of Vermont. That such reciprocal navigation and interest in the Canal, would cement and promote friendship betwixt the people of the two Canadas, and those near the Lake and the Iroquois, and would tend very much to strengthen the Treaty made betwixt Great Britain and the United States of America in 1794, under which Treaty British ships are permitted to navigate Lake Champlain for commercial purposes. That in case of war betwixt any powers, except those of Great Britain and America, the commerce of said Lake might be conveyed to Europe in 267 Vermont or British bottoms, free from capture, high insurance, or expence of convoy. Hence the enterprizing inhabitants of Vermont would find it their interest to support the government of Great Britain in Canada, whilst the remainder would be satisfied with the Canal and commerce. In peace or war, it would render the price of salt, English goods, &c. cheap, and in time of war, the exports of Vermont would bear a high price, in consequence of the ease and safety of transportation. The people of Vermont thus situated, would be averse to war ; they would, in fact, be a neutral body betwixt two great nations ; whilst their Representatives in the Legislature of the United States would oppose every idea of hostilities between Great Britain and the United States, on principles of mutual interest ; thus the most permanent contracts are established, and the blessings of peace and prosperity the rewards.

The said canal would extend navigation 180 miles into a fertile country, abounding in all kinds of iron ore, suitable to make pig-iron, bar-iron and steel, marble, white and clouded, copper and lead-mines, fir-trees* ash, white and red oaks, cedar, and various other trees. There are also a variety of rivers, with proper falls to erect iron-founderies, refineries, saw-mills, &c. where pig and bar-iron are made ; deal boards, marble

* Pine-trees in America.

slabs,

268 slabs, &c. may be sawed by water. Masts, spars, staves, &c. furnished in abundance ; of the preceding articles but little use is made for exportation. Wheat, rye, barley, Indian corn, oats, beans, pease, hemp, flax, beef, pork, butter, and cheese, are produced, in great abundance. The farmer, in clearing the timber from his lands, can furnish great supplies of charcoal to serve furnaces, refineries, &c. and furnish large quantities of ashes to make pot and pearl ashes ; these articles may be furnished cheap by the farmer, which would pay him, in many instances, for clearing his lands, instead of burning the timber on the ground to clear his lands.

A ship canal would be the means of importing salt, and exporting the preceding articles cheap ; the remittances that would be made on these raw materials would enable the merchant to make punctual remittances; it would draw commerce from the east, that now centers at Boston, Newbury Port, Portsmouth, &c. and add to the population of Lake Champlain. These measures would almost, beyond calculation, increase the commerce at both ends of said Lake, admit that heavy articles would principally pass the ship canal, yet when the reader takes into consideration the length of the river St. Lawrence, the frozen season, that goods are seldom imported but once a year to Quebec, that spring and fall shipments are seasonably made to New York, the necessity of making early 269 remittances, &c. the proprietors of the canal from Hudson's River would be benefited by said ship canal, in consequence of the extension of business ; one circumstance that would tend much to draw commerce from the east to said Lake is, that it is customary for the merchant and farmer to move most of their heavy goods and produce by sleighs, in the frozen season ; that the changeable weather on the sea coast at Boston, &c. spoils the sleigh path, so that about one journey in three are lost, while the more temperate and healthy climate of Vermont insures good sleighing for about two months.

The British merchants and manufacturers know their capitals and connexions, and that the treaty of 1794 permits them to navigate said Lake, and need not be further informed how to take the advantage of that extensive business, which is better policy than confining commerce in a narrow channel, badly calculated for the present day.

You ask me with regard to timbers ? I answer, a great variety, so great that the mere catalogue would exceed the limits of a letter. You call the oak the patriarch of the wood, and I assure you we have different species of that hardy race, the white, the black, red and swamp, all useful in civil and nautical architecture. The white pine is applied to so many uses that I can scarcely enumerate them, it may be applied to every use 270 of the deal, and the turpentine which it produces might be made a useful article of exportation. In short the trees and plants of this country

country would enrich even the Linnean system, but that must be the work of a future day ; as yet we have not discovered any gold or silver ore in this state, but if it does not boast such precious metals, it contains much more useful, such as iron, lead, copper, &c. The mineralogist would find it well worth his while to explore the very bowels of our mountains, and I am persuaded that the chymist and natural philosopher would not be disappointed in making experiments on many of the native productions in the mineral and vegetable kingdoms, and that many things which now contribute to the pride and luxury of the European countries, in colour and formation would find a rival in plants trod under foot, or minerals buried in unfrequented spots, such as red and yellow ochre, &c. putty, which even in its native state, equals in tenacity and induration the composite material of that article in your country, and employed in similar purposes.

As to your query relative to domestic animals, I feel myself able to answer you on that important head, to begin with that which is universally acknowledged to be the most useful, I mean the sheep. The breed is good, but the crossing is not studied as in England. They are remarkably prolific, the mutton sweet, and the wool generally fine and good, every farmer has a flock more or less. The breed of black cattle is daily ₂₇₁ improving, butter is good, and so is the cheese, but a few English farmers, from what I have seen, would, in a short time, bring about a surprizing change for the better in these articles ; we want a Bakewell and a Colley, and I think, if we had a few of them, in a few years we could equal the sheep walks of Lincolnshire, and the bulls of Lord Egremont, as our vegetation is at least as luxuriant and nutricious as any county in England. As to the breed of horses, it is also improving in this State, from the laudable exertion of individuals, who have learned to place a due estimate on this generous animal, either for the saddle or agriculture. I could name individuals, with pleasure, in the southern part, who have turned their attention to this article, but I do not wish to pay any personal compliment to one part, at the expence of another ; competition produces emulation, and emulation always finds its level.

I cannot help saying that it distresses me a little to think that a man of your information should seem to treat Vermout as a little sucking State, I assure you that you will find on a correct information, that even the mechanic arts are not in their infancy in this quarter, new roads are every day extending, bridges erecting, population advancing, agriculture improving, towns multiplying, and rivers marked out as objects worthy of inland navigation. We contracted no debt during the American war ; ₂₇₂ our taxes, if they can be called taxes, are light, our climate is mild, our soil fertile, our inhabitants industrous, our provisions abundant and cheap, and it is our determination to avail ourselves of these blessings, and to hand them down at least unimpaired to our children. I know

know that roads are a very important article in any country, either for
pleasure, safety, or use, the one through the medium by which neighbor-
hood and communication are kept alive and improved ; they are laid out
in as good a manner as the circumstances of the country will admit, and as
it abounds with stone, gravel, and sand, they may be rendered equal to
any in Europe ; and even in the present state, they are passable for car-
riages, &c. especially in the oldest settlements. Licensed inns are erected
on all the public roads, with good beds, a plentiful larder, and moderate bills.

Post towns are distributed over all the country, and weights and measures, leather sealers, &c. are regulated according to law, and inspected
by proper officers.

The greatest legislators from Lycurgus down to John Lock, have laid
down a moral and scientific system of education as the very foundation and cement of a State ; the Vermontese are sensible of this, and for
this purpose they have planted several public schools, and have established a university, and endowed it with funds, and academic rewards, to
draw forth and foster talents. The effects of these institutions are al-
273 ready experienced, and I trust that in a few years the rising genera-
tion will evince that these useful institutions were not laid in vain ;
remember, however, that our maxim is rather to make good men than
great scholars : let us hope for the union, for that makes the man, and
the useful citizen.

You see I have followed your queries in the order in which you ar-
ranged them ; with regard to the succession of seasons, they are by no
means sudden, as you suppose ; spring pays its welcome visit in April,
and is soon followed by summer, October and November are pleasant,
and the rest of the year is resigned to the rigid reign of winter ; too forward a spring is unfavourable, particularly if attended with a north-easterly wind, south and south-west are the rainy points ; these observations
are founded on experience and accurate meteorological observations.
The weather, however, is sometimes capricious, a fall of snow serves as
a covering to inhale the radical moisture of the earth, and as it is re-
plete with nitre, it supplies the place of manure, and when it is gradually
dissolved, vegetation shoots forth in the highest luxuriancy. With respect to seed time and harvest, spring wheat and spring rye may be sown
in April, or in May. Indian corn is planted in May, as well as barley,
oats, peas, beans, &c. Winter wheat and winter rye are sown in September and October. These are the regular seed months, but sometimes
274 they are later or earlier. Red and white clover, Timothy and other
grasses are generally sown in May and September, but not always
confined to these months. Winter wheat and winter rye are the earliest
harvest ; spring wheat, and spring rye, if sown in the last of April or
beginning

beginning of May, are cut in July or August ; Indian corn is the latest harvest, and all the rest that I have mentioned are intermediate crops.

Flax and hemp answer well in many parts. The hay harvest usually begins in July and generally ends in August, but the season is commonly favourable in that period. The produce is not gathered in with all the neatness and attention that it is in England, for to use a scripture phrase, " the harvest is great but the labourers are few," I say few comparatively speaking ; nor are the lands carried to that height of cultivation for the same reason.

The price of labour is thus raised in consequence of the scarcity of labourers ; and to use another scripture phrase, " the labourer is worthy of his hire," so that you see there is one part of the world where the reaper and the binder are held in proper degree of estimation.

You ask about the succession of crops, I shall endeavour to answer you presently on that head ; but in the first place, I must beg that you will cast your eye over the political history of the country, to which this is annexed, you will find the struggles that we were engaged in for years 275 to attain our independence. When war draws the sword, the plough-share is left to rust. When our independence was gained, our first care was to repair the devastations of war ; under these circumstances, it is not to be expected that agriculture was studied as a science. Bread, figuratively speaking, is called the staff of life ; our first care was to raise such crops as best suited with the nature of the soil, in its rude state almost ; our winter crops are rye and wheat ; our summer crops are white beans, Indian corn, summer rye and wheat, buck wheat, oats, barley, peas, flax, hemp, turnips, &c. I have touched on these things already, but my wish to give you every information, may lead me to repeat some particulars, which I hope you will excuse, for the reasons I have just mentioned ; I shall only add, that such is the certainty of the seasons, that all these crops, if sown and planted in due time, seldom fail to repay the toil and expence of the husbandman.

As to gardening, it has been attended to pretty much of late, but I cannot say that it is in that advanced state which you wish, and of which it is certainly capable, from climate, situation and soil. There is a garden, however, annexed to every house, always well stored with pulse and roots for the supply of the table ; parsnips, carrots, turnips, cabbage, potatoes, pumpkins, &c. grow in such abundance, that we begin to fatten 276 swine with them. A swine is said to be the only animal that is found from pole to pole, capable of contending with rattle-snakes, and their poison free of danger. As soon as the acorns, beech-nuts, &c. begin to fall, they are driven to the woods, in large herds, to feed on them. The delicacy, taste, and nutrition of these nuts are particularly
suited

suited to the palate of these animals, so that in a short time they grow to a great size. The hog prefers the beech nut to any other, and the effect of that preference is visible in growth and fat, hence a good beech nut year may be called a good swine year. At a proper period they are prepared for the knife, this is done by giving them a certain quantity of sulphur, and when it has sufficiently operated, they are then fed with Indian corn or meal, which render their flesh firmer than any other food. We have no windmills, nor is there any occasion for them in a country so well watered. Corn or grist mills are every day erecting, a proof of the advancement of agriculture. Mill stones are found in almost every part of the country. Sumach grows in great plenty over all the state, and of the finest quality too. It is hoped that one day it will be turned to more use than it is at present.

I have abstained from entering into the natural history of Vermont, as it would lead into a wide field. The butter nut tree, however, should be mentioned, I think it may be classed as a species of the walnut ; it bears an immense quantity of nuts, in clusters, the size of a hen's-egg each. 277 They make excellent pickle, and when pressed or boiled, produce great quantities of oil, which is of a sanative quality, in rheumatism, &c. The bark of this tree is used in dying black, which preserves a fine jetty gloss for a long time ; wainscotting are sometimes formed of the wood. The cows in winter are fed with hay, clover, turnips, pumpkins, &c. Those that give milk in that season are fed with oats, Indian corn, ground together and mixed with wheat bran.

Marl is found in many parts of Vermont, but as the ground is fertile and in good heart, it is not used as a manure, but it is probable that it will be found very useful in that line hereafter, when on sandy grounds, &c. as sand is good on marly ground. Lime stone is also abundant, and I need not tell you that it is an excellent manure. Maple sugar forms a great article of domestic consumption, the material is plenty, the preparation is easy, the taste agreeable, it seldom cloys the stomach, it is an excellent anti-scorbutic, and so innocent, that it may be taken in almost any quantity by infants.

I cannot say that we have any birds that are not common to the other States, such as the swallow, woodcock, quail, &c.

Notwithstanding I have said that every farmer is in some respect a mechanic, you should take it as I intended it, rather a general expression, for there are handicrafts who find encouragement enough to apply 278 to particular trades, without so much as scarce ever putting the hand to the plough, such as smiths, taylors, carpenters, shoemakers, &c. they find employment enough, and in a few years I am persuaded that the

the manual arts will become more visible and distinct, and that one man will not be found to trench on the business of another, but at the same time that all will be thrown open to merit, industry, and perseverance ; and that the State, like a well regulated machine, will be composed of different members, and every one in it's place.

You wish to know which is the usual and best mode of travelling, I have told you already that our roads are rather indifferent. The usual mode is on horse back, but of late stage coaches are established, and the fare is moderate, the inn-keepers civil, and the entertainment good. In winter, when the roads are rendered good by the frost, we travel in sleighs, as in Sweden, Denmark, &c.

I scarce know of any nation that pays a greater deference to the fair sex than the Americans, and very deservedly too, for it is but justice to my fair country-women to say, that they are highly worthy of it in every situation, maid, wife and widow. Their education is virtuous, and suited to the line in which fortune has destined they should move, thus every woman thinks it sufficient to shine in her own domestic sphere. The men willingly assume all the toils of the field, and every species of servile labour. Women are employed in the concerns of the house, 279 such as preparing the frugal repast, spinning, weaving, knitting, &c. sometimes they assist in binding the sheaves, or other light labours in the harvest. Every mother generally nurses her own child, unless through bodily infirmity. The winter nights are passed in reading rustic jokes and tales. Dancing is a favourite amusement in this season.

I know you will be pleased to hear that that art, which is the conservatrix of all others, printing, is encouraged and protected ; four or five newspapers are printed in this State, and have a circulation ; several useful books are also printed, as the laudable passion for reading is daily encreasing. You seem to be very much alarmed at the bare mention of the rattle-snake, and I am not surprized at it, from the frightful accounts of modern travellers, permit me to say a word or two on this reptile. The rattle-snakes, in the early frosts about the month of October, retire to craggy rocks, where they find some subterraneous cavity, in which they remain in a state of torpor till the return of spring, when they crawl forth ; at this season they are not poisonous, as they are too feeble, and their venom is not sufficiently concocted till they drink water, which ferments and increases the virus. Their dens or haunts are sought for the purpose of destroying them, as their grease is valuable in many medical cases, which is an incentive to trace and destroy them, so that they 280 are diminished in proportion as the country is cultivated and cleared.

And

And as it seems to be a dictate in nature that there is no bane for which there is not a remedy, the Indians are in possession of one, and can effectually cure their bite ; nor is the secret confined to them alone. The swine eat or feed on them, this also tends to lessen their number, so that at present they are to be found in very few places in Vermont; these plain facts I hope will quiet your fears.

Pot and pearl ash form at present no inconsiderable article of export and home consumption.

Our Vermontese house-wives are not a little vain of their knowledge in making home-made wines, such as gooseberry, rasberry, &c. these native productions are exceedingly pleasing, refreshing, and healthy.

Cyder is a favorite beverage, the flavor is fine, of a proper age it sparkles and mantles in the glass ; it is found to be an excellent anti-scorbutic, and if used for a certain period, corrects impurities of the blood.

Some lead-mines have been discovered of late, and I doubt not, when the naturalists and mineralogists explore those regions, that they will 281 discover many treasures in their respective lines highly estimable at this day in Europe in the materia medica, dying, building, ornament and use.

Hats are composed of beaver, and manufactured by the inhabitants. Felt hats are also worn and manufactured in the State.

Inocculation has been introduced with great success, and by this means thousands of lives are preserved to the community. The meazles are not so dangerous as heretofore, as the treatment of this disorder has deprived it in a great degree of its malignity.

You ask what manufactures would thrive best in Vermont ? I am persuaded the difficulty would be to point out the manufactory that would not flourish in it.

Thus I have attempted to give you a short but faithful answer to your queries ; if you favour this country with a visit, you will find that I have only failed in one thing, and that is, that my descriptive powers cannot do justice to the fertility and beauty of the country, to the hospitality of its inhabitants, to the plenty that is found in every house, and the content that is pictured in every countenance, and that reigns in every heart—would that all mankind were as happy this minute as the Vermontese.

INDEX TO ALLEN'S HISTORY

A.

B.

C.

M.

N.

Y.

974.3 A11

Allen, Ira.

DATE DUE	
MAY 23 '12	
JUN 22 '12	
GAYLORD	PRINTED IN U.S.A.

Richmond Free Library
P.O. Box 997
201 Bridge St.
Richmond, VT 05477
434-3036